Growing Your
HOME-BASED
BUSINESS

A Complete Guide to Proven Sales & Marketing Strategies

KIM T. GORDON

PRENTICE HALL
Englewood Cliffs, New Jersey 07632

Prentice-Hall International (UK) Limited, *London*
Prentice-Hall of Australia Pty. Limited, *Sydney*
Prentice-Hall Canada, Inc., *Toronto*
Prentice-Hall Hispanoamericana, S.A., *Mexico*
Prentice-Hall of India Private Limited, *New Delhi*
Prentice-Hall of Japan, Inc., *Tokyo*
Simon & Schuster Asia Pte. Ltd., *Singapore*
Editora Prentice-Hall do Brasil, Ltda., *Rio de Janeiro*

©1992 *by*
Kim T. Gordon

10 9 8 7 6 5 4 3 2 1

Library of Congress Cataloging-in-Publication Data

Gordon, Kim T.
  Growing your home-based business : a complete guide to proven
sales and marketing communication strategies / Kim T. Gordon.
      p.   c.m.
    Includes index.
    ISBN 0-13-366170-9
    1. Home-based businesses—United States. 2. New business
enterprises—United States. 3. Marketing.   I. Title.
HD2336.U5G68   1993   92-20498
658.8—dc20   CIP

ISBN 0-13-366170-9

PRENTICE HALL
Professional Publishing
Englewood Cliffs, NJ 07632
Simon & Schuster. A Paramount Communications Company

Printed in the United States of America

How This Book Will Help You

There's no place like home. When history looks back on the 1990s, it will undoubtedly show a mass exodus from traditional workplaces—the corporation, factory, and storefront business—as American workers by the millions choose to stay home and work. To many, it's the 1990s equivalent of living over the store. While to others, it's the starting place from which to grow a future Fortune 500 company. No matter what your goals or philosophies, being a home-based business owner carries with it the opportunity to reap enormous rewards—provided you are prepared to master the skills required to grow your new company. For most home-based business owners, the greatest challenge lies in formulating and executing strategies for promoting their businesses and increasing sales.

Growing Your Home Based Business is a complete sales and marketing communications guide to home-based business success. It provides the same fundamental strategies and techniques used by sales and marketing experts. You'll discover how to increase the income from your home-based business while preserving and perpetuating all the benefits you and your family enjoy as a result of your new lifestyle and workstyle. Even if you are a new or would-be home-based entrepreneur, the strategies in this book will guide you, step by step, past the most common and costly sales and marketing mistakes that often lead to new business failure.

The benefits of home-based ownership are enormous. You can earn more money, gain greater freedom and flexibility, increase enjoyment of your work, gain family time, greatly reduce stress, and more. But becoming a home-based business owner also means going it alone, without the support of a larger organization. Now *you* are the individual responsible for the long-range success of your venture. Sales and marketing communications activities must become an essential part of your routine.

In the coming chapters, you'll explore a series of proven methods of increasing income from your home-based business. You will:

- Discover techniques for positioning your company
- Create sales and marketing communications messages that motivate prospects
- Master the basics of lead generation for consistent, stable new business year-round
- Gain insight into the methods used by top salespeople for successfully guiding and closing sales transactions
- Develop a sophisticated, high-quality company image
- Avoid costly media buying mistakes and
- Create action plans that work hard to keep your business and budgets on track.

Growing Your Home-Based Business gives you the tools you need to successfully build your company's sales. You too can reap the benefits enjoyed by knowledgeable business owners across the country who are increasing their incomes and gaining greater enjoyment of their lives and work while growing their home-based businesses.

A Word From the Author

Some years ago, when I decided to create and build my own company, basing it in my home seemed an ideal solution. At the time, I chose to leave the position of vice president of marketing at a firm which, with the aid of my strategies and programs, had just reached the apex of its growth—$2.5 billion in sales. And much of what I liked and disliked about my position there had an impact on my choices when structuring and locating my new business.

While the work itself had been challenging and enormously interesting, I was fed up with the twice daily, hour-and-a-half commute to the main office (plus travel to the sixty-two regional sales offices) and the debilitating political infighting at the seniormost level. I remembered what it had been like to work as director of development of a small marketing communications company—before we grew it from 18 people to 120 people in just over four years. This was where one could see teamwork pay off in quality work and personal satisfaction.

I decided my new business would be structured to start small and stay small (although we would increase in income and profitability each year), drawing on the creativity and expertise of a handful of top people and a larger network of affiliated individuals and companies as needed. By basing my new company in my home, I would avoid the tedious commute I'd come to dislike and keep my overhead low and profits high.

Thanks to a structured sales and marketing communications effort, plus a network of professionals who provided referrals, my very first year in operation provided a higher income than I had ever had working for someone else. And there have been a number of other pluses. An addition on our home was renovated to include spacious, bright office space and an adjoining bath which open onto a lovely, tranquil shade garden of my own design. To me, this is a step closer to heaven than a corner office in any high-rise, glass-enclosed office building.

Being home-based allows me to focus on my work without interruption and with great intensity for longer periods of time. Simply put, a lot more work gets done. Higher income, less stress, greater enjoyment of life, and freedom to focus on quality work have been the immediate, positive attributes of my home-based business.

But there have been negative and surprising consequences as well. I was poorly prepared for the perceived drop in "status." While this is likely to occur upon leaving any high-profile position, becoming home-based, however, seemed to lead some people to the conclusion that I was simply "hanging around the house." This was in spite of my apparent success at entrepreneurship and personal satisfaction in being home-based. When a national business magazine profiled my company and business philosophy, the otherwise excellent interview was headlined, "Home Based and Still a Business."

Fortunately, the outdated perceptions implied by that headline have not deterred the millions like myself who refuse to be shackled by outmoded business ideas. And reading beyond the headline, that article struck a positive chord in many readers who were motivated to call me to discuss their own home-based businesses. Nearly all sought advice on building sales and growing their companies. And it was this input from home-based business owners from across the country which convinced me to write this book.

The characters in the book are not real people. Instead, they're compilations, all with fictitious names. In this way, stories of many successes and a few failures can be presented without damaging businesses, reputations, or feelings. In some instances, cases have been combined to provide well-rounded examples. Resemblance to any real individuals is not intended.

Many thanks go to my husband, Stephen Mizner, for his feedback while writing this book, and to my family, good friends, and associates for their encouragement. And I reserve special thanks for all the home-based business owners and would-be home-based entrepreneurs who have requested the information and guidance in this book. Here's to your success!

Kim T. Gordon

Contents

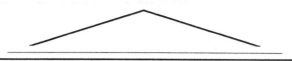

chapter one

How to Sell What Your Prospects Want to Buy

The movement toward working at home is changing the face of American business. Across the nation, accountants, salespeople, business executives, architects, contractors, advertising and public relations practitioners, publishers, computer specialists, childcare workers, consultants, artisans and countless others are becoming home-based business owners.

Many begin without the technical sales and marketing expertise they'll need to generate a continuing stream of new business—the lifeblood of any growing company. Take Linda K., who went to work right out of college for a small publishing company, worked her way up the ladder as an editor and, after nine years, into senior management of a mid-sized publishing firm.

When Linda decided to open her own newsletter publishing company based in her home, she was confident and capable. She had exactly the expertise she needed to begin a publishing business—with one exception. Her technical and managerial experience did not include the essential sales skills necessary to initiate contact with prospects, guide a sales transaction or structure an ongoing sales program.

For Linda, creating her group of marketing tools was a snap. But when it came time to use those tools effectively to support a sales effort, such as buying advertising space or deciding the frequency of her direct mail campaign, she was at a loss and knew she'd need some help.

Like Linda, Richard H., a veteran association president with 22 years experience, is highly expert in professional association management. Yet when he founded his own association management firm, he discovered the greatest challenge lay not in building his clients' association memberships, but in expanding his own client roster.

Today, few companies can survive without plans and programs for effective promotion. Indeed, a small client roster leaves the home-based business owner more vulnerable to financial loss than the broader client base customarily managed by larger, out-of-home based firms. And competition is heating up. Even as the soaring numbers of home-based businesses positively affects their image and overall acceptability, survival increasingly requires strong development skills.

Unifying Messages for Effective Promotion

The world will learn about your home-based business in one of two ways, either through sales activities or marketing communications.

Sales activities involve interpersonal contact which moves a prospect closer to a buying decision. The term *marketing* has many broad applications and generally includes everything from pricing and distribution to communications. The more specific, technical term *marketing communications* applies solely to the communications tools and methods used to market your company to the target audiences.

As a home-based business owner, you have a tremendous advantage in your ability to control, tailor, and integrate all sales and marketing communications messages until they have the power to motivate prospects. Through unification of all sales and marketing communications messages, you help insure achievement of your goals by repeatedly reinforcing the key selling points in everything which is said, heard, or seen concerning your company's products or services.

During the years she spent working as a salesperson for a large, national wholesale distribution company, Susan B. became extremely familiar with the consequences of a company's failure to effectively unify sales and marketing communications messages and strategies. Year after year, Susan and her fellow field sales representatives found themselves selling customers one set of benefits and special product offers long after their company had launched yet another new advertising and direct marketing program promoting an entirely different group of benefits and offers. Not only did this result in a deep sense of frustration for Susan and her co-workers, but also, more critically, it resulted in lost sales and revenues nationwide.

Now Susan is president of her own small, highly successful, wholesale distribution company. As a home-based business owner, she is closer to her market than her past employer, now her competitor, can ever be. She has tailored her company's messages to meet the ongoing needs of customers and prospects, and she has integrated sales and marketing communications to consistently reinforce key selling points. It's no wonder Susan's firm continues to steadily build sales of the product lines it represents.

Positioning to Meet the Needs of Your Target Audience

Judy K. had been designing and creating unique, exquisite jewelry for over a decade. Her highly original creations combined gold and fine gemstones in current, often groundbreaking designs. For the past three years, she had been employed as a designer in a fine jewelry store located in an upscale mall frequented by a wealthy and discerning customer base.

Although Judy earned praise and yearly raises from the store's owners and her work became increasingly popular with customers, over time she became frustrated. She felt weighed down by her lack of autonomy and limited opportunities for advancement and she was dissatisfied with her income, which, despite the popularity of her work, still hovered around $30,000 per year.

Not surprisingly, Judy decided to put all of her talents and expertise to the test by opening her own jewelry design and manufacturing business. She chose to base the new company in the light-filled studio in the back of her townhouse on a quiet suburban street. In the first three months, business was steady and promising. Judy sold her contemporary gold and gemstone jewelry to friends and neighbors as well as to the store where she had been previously employed. She soon hired an assistant to work with her in the home studio three days per week.

Several months later, Judy participated in a local arts and crafts show with marginal results. Research and forethought would have shown her that the demographics of those attending this particular show did not match the established profile of her upscale, affluent buyer. And without having prepared her display to target the show's less affluent shoppers, she stood idly by as her $900–$1,200 necklaces remained in their cases while a jewelry designer in the adjoining booth sold out of $200 silver rings.

Within six to eight months of opening her own design firm it became clear that in order to grow the business, Judy would have to sell her work to prominent local jewelry stores, chains, and department stores. Armed with her newest and best collection, Judy made visits to two jewelry store buyers in the same upscale mall where she been previously employed. Both presentations fell flat. This was a disaster, falling so close on the heels of the craft show failure.

While both buyers had been intrigued by the beauty and uniqueness of her designs, neither would make a commitment or even show much enthusiasm for carrying her line. Clearly, the problem was not with the product line itself. Judy's work was continuing to sell well in another store in the same mall. The problem lay in Judy's failure to understand the basic difference between what she had to sell and what her prospects—in this case the store buyers—wanted to buy.

Charles Revson, founder of Revlon, one of America's most successful companies, is reported to have said, "In the factories we make cosmetics. In the stores we sell hope."

Judy showed a bright, beautiful product line to qualified prospects. Yet she met with disaster because she failed to position her product so as to meet the needs of her target audience. Features are the tangible characteristics of a company's products or services. Benefits are what all prospects hope to derive through use of those products or services.

The pieces designed and manufactured by Judy and her assistant are "14 karat gold in a matte finish with no less than two high quality gemstones each." These are key features. The features become powerful motivators when translated into benefits her store buyer prospects can easily relate to. She might have offered, "Proven contemporary design which will have the highest appeal to your affluent, frequent customers. Our colored gemstone designs offer the opportunity for repeat sales to the same customer as she may buy a number of pieces to coordinate with different color outfits."

How to Use Benefits to Motivate Prospects

Translating what it is you have to sell, the features of your product or service, into benefits your target audience can easily relate to is simple once you understand the prospects' needs and expectations. Benefits, not features, motivate our prospects to take action. No sales presentation, no ad, no corporate brochure can be successful without focusing on those benefits the target audience wants, expects to receive, and is prepared to pay for.

By translating features into benefits we come up with the answer to why customers will want to buy from us. This becomes the crux of our selling message or, more technically, the sales and marketing communications platform from which all sales and marketing messages will emanate. Your sales and marketing communications platform, when fully developed, should be no longer than one page or several short paragraphs. In fact, the more concise the better. Or, if your company has a wide range of target audiences, you'll develop a corresponding number of platforms by which all verbal and written communications will be guided.

With fifteen years experience in mid-sized accounting firms, Mark B. had risen to the level of vice president in a highly successful downtown firm. Working with large corporate clients, he had become adept at zeroing in on client problem areas and recommending clear solutions for restructuring and realigning both the systems and personnel. But day after day he began to feel a certain sameness to his job and saw his long nights and weekends of work yielding little opportunity of earning him the corporation's number one slot—that is unless he was prepared to put in another fifteen years at the firm.

Mark decided to open his own accounting company, keeping his expenses and overhead low by converting his family's old rec room at home into a professional office. With a separate entrance (formerly a back door used primarily to keep his children from muddying up the front hall) and adjacent bathroom, this location proved ideal. And he was quickly set up with computer, answering equipment, fax machine, and all the accoutrements of today's high-tech office. He also arranged a clerical relationship with a secretarial service nearby and contracted for additional accounting support services through his many contacts in the field.

Within thirty days, Mark was handling the accounting for a small business owned by an old college friend, and he was busy dreaming up ways of securing new accounts. He quickly wrote a small newspaper advertisement and his own brochure, then had the brochure typeset and quick printed at a shop nearby. Mark was confident his ad and brochure would drum up the additional business he needed to get his new firm off and running.

The short laundry list of copy points made in the two pieces included:

- Fifteen years experience in major accounting firms
- Comprehensive accounting software and management analysis
- Specialization in small and mid-sized companies
- Complete tax and corporate financial planning available

Much to Mark's surprise, the brochure drew lukewarm responses from the first fifty prospects. Follow-up calls to several key prospect companies revealed he had failed to move them from complacency, and they chose to remain with their existing accounting companies. His ad pulled even worse, though well placed, timed, and cleanly executed by the local newspaper.

As with Judy's verbal presentations, Mark's written communications failed to translate features into benefits and consequently failed to either create or fill prospects' needs.

Creating a Unique Message

Defining your own sales and marketing communications platform can help you avoid this common failure among new business owners. This simple exercise will enable you to isolate and clearly identify what you have to sell (the special features of your product or service); the benefits prospects want, expect to receive, and are prepared to pay for (the key benefits they expect to derive); and the distinction between what you sell and the products or services offered by your competition.

Simply take a sheet of paper and draw a vertical line down the center. Write the heading "Features" above the left column and the heading "Benefits" at the top of the right column, as shown in the examples for Judy's jewelry business and Mark's accounting firm. List all the key features of your company, its products or services on the left, being certain to list any features which make your company unique or distinct from the competition. Be sure to include all characteristics. This list will be quite long and may fill the entire left side of your page.

Once you have listed all the key features of your firm, begin translating those features into benefits in the column on the right. In many cases, several features will translate into one single benefit. It helps to put yourself in your prospect's shoes and ask yourself, "What does he or she need from me?"

Benefits to be derived are sometimes quite obvious and may include making money, saving money, and other tangible benefits. Intangible benefits are important too, such as looking good to one's superiors by hiring the right public relations firm or feeling secure that one's child will be safe and sound all day through selection of an excellent child-care center.

The two examples which follow show how to use this exercise to help translate features to benefits.

1. Judy's Jewelry

Features	Benefits
Unique, contemporary design	Appeals to most affluent, trend
Variety in color and shape	setting customers
Colored gemstones and gold	Potential for repeat sales to your best
Popular with affluent shoppers	customers
Low overhead	Enhances your store's image through
Product has limited exposure	cutting-edge design
Experienced in quality manufacture	Low cost to you means higher store
Can easily produce new and exclusive	profit
lines	No financial risk with stock offered on
Coordinated look in earrings,	consignment or trial
necklaces, rings, and bracelets	Exclusive lines may be sold at a
A loyal customer following	premium
Local manufacture	Opportunity for large individual sales
Can quickly fill special orders	of matching pieces
	Will bring in new customers
	Few, if any, returns for repair
	Free repair
	Custom orders yield large profits
	High customer satisfaction thanks to
	quick response on special orders

2. Mark's Accounting

Features	Benefits
Small client base	Receive highly responsive,
Can recommend and upgrade	personalized attention
accounting software	Improve cash on hand/cash flow
Can analyze and streamline systems	Reduce time it takes to bill customers
Will analyze personnel requirements	and process receivables
Performs accounting functions off-site	Save money on systems and personnel
Subcontracts day-to-day tasks	Allocate and manage funds for stable
Can work with small and mid-sized	growth and expansion
companies	Increase shareholder revenues
Offers financial planning for	Reduce your overhead with fewer
companies and senior execs	in-house, non-billable employees
Performs corporate tax planning	Accumulate and protect your
and prep	personal wealth
Low overhead	Save money on taxes
Fifteen years experience	Maximize deductions
Flexible compensation	Reduce accounting costs thanks to
Understands the needs of large	affordable services
corporations	

Answering the Question, What's in It for Me?

By now, the right-hand column of your page should contain a comprehensive list of benefits your customers or clients may derive by using your product or service. Before moving on to create your completed platform, take a final, careful look at those benefits. Are they measurably or discernibly different from those benefits to be derived by using your competitors' products or services? Do they meet the needs of your prospects? Do you present benefits which your target audiences are prepared to pay for?

If not, go back and have a second look at your product or service itself as well as such factors as pricing, quality, level of service, and delivery. In order to survive and prosper, your home-based business must do so without the added strength of a well-known corporate entity, a large, attractive storefront or high profile suite in an executive office building. The merits of your business' products or services, coupled with your ability to position your company and sell benefits to qualified prospects, will become three of the most critical factors in gaining new business.

Once confident your product or service itself and its resulting benefits will stimulate the target audience to action, it is time to formulate a final sales and marketing communications platform. This is accomplished by simplifying your list of benefits until it is distilled into a group of phrases to which the target audience can easily relate.

Your completed platform will contain more than one series of benefit statements as not all types of prospects want, expect to receive, and are prepared to pay for the same things. In cases where you must market to widely different target audiences with products whose benefits differ, more than one sales and marketing communications platform will be needed.

Two Model Sales and Marketing Communications Platforms

To help you evaluate the structure and content of your own newly created platform, here are two completed examples.

Judy's Jewelry

Judy's fine jewelry combines unique contemporary design with fine gemstones and 14K gold to create pieces which appeal to your most affluent, trend-setting customers. A proven product line, Judy's jewelry brings with it an upscale customer base.

Our colored gemstone designs offer the opportunity for repeat sales to the same customer as she may purchase a number of pieces to coordinate with different color wardrobes. In addition to repeat sales, large dollar transactions are not uncommon as purchasers choose earrings, rings, necklaces, and bracelets to complete each look.

Judy's Jewelry will work with you to create an exclusive store line which will complement and enhance your store's image. Thanks to local design and manufacture, custom design and special order pieces are quickly produced to your exact specifications. Unlike contemporary jewelry produced in Italy or New York, local manufacture means lower cost to you and higher store profit. And our quality is fully guaranteed.

Mark's Accounting

Mark's accounting firm is a highly specialized accounting and financial planning company focused on the financial success of your small or mid-sized business. Through personalized attention to your day-to-day business accounting needs, Mark's accounting helps you to save money on systems and personnel, to improve cash flow, to reduce overhead and processing time for billing and receivables, and to increase shareholder revenues.

Thanks to affordable tax and financial planning services for your company, yourself, and other senior executives, you can accumulate and protect your personal wealth, save money on taxes by maximizing deductions, and allocate funds for stable corporate growth and expansion. Whether your company's needs include systems, personnel, or software management, Mark's accounting firm provides money-saving solutions to your financial challenges.

As the preceeding examples show, to be effective your sales and marketing communications platform must answer the prospect's question, What's in it for me? Your newly created platform will become the solid foundation upon which all future written and verbal communications are built.

How To Monitor Your Customers' Needs

Over time, your clients' or customers' needs and desires may change. So, to sell what they want to buy on an ongoing basis will require continual monitoring and periodic adjustment of your sales and marketing communications platform.

There are two principal means for monitoring your customers' or clients' needs and desires:

- competitive intelligence
- customer analysis

Gathering Competitive Intelligence

You don't have to be Sherlock Holmes to stay abreast of competitive information. It just takes a bit of time and diligence. First, identify the principal publications your target audience reads for information about your type of product or service. Then acquire subscriptions or regularly purchase those publications to scan the editorial matter and the advertising. Look closely at all the competitive advertising to identify what appear to be the industry-wide key selling points. These would be features or benefits which are touted in a number of ads. A strong similarity of key selling points among competitors throughout your industry or market is a clear indication of the benefits all prospects will expect to derive from use of your type of product or service. Look closely at the advertising of your principal competition. And, if necessary, revise your sales and marketing communications platform to include benefits which are in some ways superior to those of your competitors so that you can effectively position against them.

Even if your principal competitors do not advertise, it's still necessary to read the publications your target audience looks to for information; the editorial itself will provide insight to their needs and desires. Further, articles may be written about companies with whom you compete or about industry leaders that set the standard by which the benefits of your own product or service will be judged.

Another means for gathering competitive intelligence is to "mystery shop." Respond to your competitors' ads just as a prospect might. Or telephone them and request literature. By reviewing competitive literature or by going so far as to take a sales call from one of your competitors, you'll gain valuable insight into their sales and marketing communications messages and the way they treat their customers. Of course, gathering competitive literature is an important step not only in formulating your sales and marketing communications platform and in fine-tuning it along the way, but also as a preliminary step to developing your own family of sales and marketing communications materials.

After you have gathered literature from all your chief competitors, evaluate the materials, looking for similarities as well as differences. For example, do the majority of competitors use #10 size brochures, or are four-color folders with inserts preferred? Is there a uniformity of messages? What niches have key competitors sought to develop? And can you—or should you—position your business directly against these competitors, or should you develop a unique niche of your own?

In addition to reviewing your competitors' literature, you may also be in a position to buy and examine their products. If so, compare quality, pricing, delivery, and customer service to see how your own product stacks up against them.

For many home-based business owners competing in less tangible service arenas, mystery shopping is more difficult. In this case, it may be helpful to include talks with suppliers in your competitive intelligence-gathering efforts. Suppliers are often in a position to have a great deal of information concerning the internal workings of your competitors, ranging from the kind of people they are to work with to whether they pay their bills on time. This kind of general information can be obtained in normal conversation and should never be forced or coerced from a supplier—or he might say a few unkind words about you to your competitors.

Business luncheons, association meetings, and all manner of professional opportunities for networking can also be excellent places to meet and learn more about your competition. In short, getting to know your competitors and their sales and marketing communications messages is vitally important to understanding the expectations of your target audience members and what they will wish to buy from you.

How To Fine-Tune Your Message with Customer Research and Analysis

No matter what your business or industry, no doubt hundreds of pages of research information already exist concerning the profile of your customer base and what, how, and when they are motivated to buy. Never assume, because you have been working in your field for a number of years, that it's unnecessary to review published research information. A single product innovation or something as subtle as a minor change in the economy can trigger enormous changes in your target audience's expectations and desire to buy. Your periodic review of published data is essential to staying abreast or ahead of the trends. Such data is easily available through on-line data services or directly from trade or other publications, newsletters, and national associations.

Mark accesses his on-line data service approximately once a month to gain ideas from published articles on strategies for marketing his accounting services. He has gained some important information on what owners of small businesses look for from financial planners. But it's not necessary to have services on-line in your own office to access this information. Database research companies proliferate and most, for a minimum fee and an hourly charge, will provide data searches on specific topics or questions for you.

You can also gather information directly from its source, such as by contacting the trade publications read by your target prospect groups for copies of any readership or other studies concerning the buying habits of your audiences. These studies and related information are readily available to advertisers in trade publications and, in many cases, to others as well.

National trade and professional associations often commission studies and regularly compile information of special interest to their members, including, of course, marketing information. Judy uses information gleaned from published studies from a national association in order to fine-tune her sales and marketing communications platform to meet the needs and expectations of her primary target audience, the store buyers. She also uses information from the same studies to help determine how her product lines should change over time in order to satisfy the desires of the jewelry store customers for new and exciting designs. Her research has also shown what percentage of the jewelry-buying market will purchase her type of gemstone creations. And Judy uses this information to refine her sales approach to stores which most closely cater to that particular type of jewelry customer.

In addition to secondary research (examination of published articles and facts), primary research can play a part in examining what your own unique customer base wants to buy. To many home-based business owners with few, if any, dollars budgeted for research, simple customer analysis, such as customer surveys, questionnaires, and comment cards, provide an excellent means for acquiring proprietary data without the assistance of outside research firms.

Analysis may begin soon after your home-based business has established a small customer or client base. Early on, use these tools to validate your basic assumptions concerning your client or buyer profile. Demographic, geographic, or business and professional criteria should be verified. Depending upon your type of business, the information you require will vary. For example, age, sex, and income are important when profiling a customer for a consumer product, while business title, size, and type of company are important when examining the client base of your business product or service company.

No matter what your type of business, be certain to ask all customers and clients where they get general information on your type of product or service. Determine their buying habits, satisfaction with your product or service, and, of course, what your customers or clients believe their future needs may be. Overall, it's most critical to determine whether your own product or service meets their expectations.

Another use for these valuable customer analysis tools is to gain input for marketing communications and sales. Once your home-based business is more mature, test which of your media vehicles are best remembered. Also consider asking your clients or customers to provide comments and names of referrals. You may choose to mail a customer survey as a follow-up. Brief comment cards may be included in business product packaging, or a short questionnaire may be completed by telephone.

Make your customer/client analysis tools easy and quick to use. Provide boxes or spaces where answers may be checked off, and never expect all but the most motivated customers to provide lengthy written answers. And most important—be certain your customers or clients know this information is being gathered to help you better serve their needs in the future. Analysis or research should never be confused with a sales pitch, or you may find your customers or clients unwilling to cooperate.

If more in-depth information concerning your customer or client base is required—and if funds are available for research—you may wish to consider employing a professional research firm. Indeed, this may be essential to your success if you plan to sell a consumer product of any type on a regional or national basis. And the launch of any new or unique business product or service can also benefit significantly from testing.

The types of services typically performed by skilled research firms include in-depth interviews, mail surveys, telephone surveys, focus groups, central location studies (such as surveys in shopping malls), and market area research. Research firms handle both qualitative analysis (how prospects or customers think or feel about something) and quantitative analysis (for example, the number of individuals within a geographic market area who fit your target audience profile). Research costs will vary depending upon what is being tested and the methods employed. Naturally, the larger the test, the more costly the analysis.

In all, to successfully sell what your customers or clients want to buy requires development and continual modification and adjustment of a sales and marketing communications platform. And your platform must speak directly to the benefits prospects will derive by using your product or service. By learning as much as you can about your clients or customers and the expectations raised by your competition, you will dramatically increase your company's success with targeted prospects.

chapter two

How To Target Prospects With a Proactive Sales Program

It's a simple business truth. Consistent, proactive, well-targeted sales activities are an essential component of steady, long-range business growth. As a new home-based business owner with limited or no support staff, you may be tempted to engage in sales activities only when there is little other work—simply in the "slow" times. But beware: You could be condemning yourself and your family to life on an economic roller coaster.

Acquiring new business requires consistent sales activities over a period of months and years. By creating your own sales program to generate new business, you prevent crucial sales activities from falling by the wayside. The key is to assemble a program which you can easily manage along with the day-to-day operations of your growing company.

In addition to being consistent, the program you devise must be proactive—one which you initiate, drive, and essentially control. You'll never see a successful home-based entrepreneur sitting by the phone like a hopeful teenager, waiting for it to ring.

Emanuel A., president of a home-based translation/language service, never saw the need for a proactive marketing program until there were senior-level personnel changes at the embassy which had provided the majority of his business for nearly its first full year. Had he established a proactive new business program from his company's inception, he would have spared himself and his family months of lean times while he frantically struggled to devise a prospect list, initiate contact with new prospects, and close several small accounts. Now, Emanuel relies on his proactive sales program and consistently sets aside several hours each week for sales.

Save Time and Money Through Target Marketing

A sales program which is well targeted reaches out to your best prospects, those who are most likely to desire and be willing to pay for those benefits your product or service can deliver. All sales and marketing communications programs (as seen in Chapter 9) must be finely crafted to target narrow prospect groups.

Target marketing will save you time. With a limited number of hours per week for sales activities, there's little time to waste on marginal or unqualified prospect groups. And target marketing will save you money on everything from billable hours to postage and printing of sales tools. But most important, a well-targeted sales program will dramatically increase the likelihood of success for your new business.

The structure of your sales program, though not the skills you will need to employ it, will vary depending upon whether you are marketing a product or service. The first consideration is whether you will be selling to other businesses or directly to consumers.

Business-to-Business Sales ───────────────

How To Build Comprehensive Prospect Lists

Business-to-business sales programs for services and most products generally involve initiation of one-on-one sales contact, either by telephone, in person, or both. The exceptions would be some business products, such as low-cost software, office supplies, and educational tools, among others. These may be sold through marketing communications alone; by using advertising and direct mail, for example.

Building an effective sales program to target key prospects starts with developing comprehensive prospect lists. Initially, all new prospect lists will be developed through research. Later, they will be expanded to include qualified prospects gleaned from lead generation activities, such as advertising and public relations, and prior contacts.

If you are selling to other businesses, you will begin by narrowing your target audiences by such factors as geographic market area and type of business, industry, or profession. Other qualifying factors, from size of business and length of time in operation through creditworthiness, may be important to you. If so, these qualifications should be considered when developing your lists. It's easiest to start from the most general characteristics and weed out less desirable prospects with more specific criteria.

Cynthia and Alex S. are a husband-and-wife public relations team operating, with the help of a part-time office manager, from a large home office. Cynthia and Alex used their prior experience to help them define the prospect categories for their new home-based business. They then made some decisions concerning their preferred lifestyle and client base and began to draw up prospect lists accordingly.

In order to develop an effective prospect list, Cynthia and Alex each categorized their public relations experience by industry. Cynthia, whose work had been focused on special promotions, listed builder/developers, hotels, restaurants, retail stores, financial institutions, and shopping malls. Alex, whose experience centered primarily on corporate public relations, listed banking, chemical processing, housing, beverage manufacturing, and paper products.

The areas in which their categories overlapped became their primary targets, as account work in those areas would allow them to capitalize on their mutual strengths and to pitch and work as a team. For example, Alex could handle the overall public relations for a large residential housing developer while Cynthia might create and manage special promotional events for launching each new home subdivision. Those categories in which their experiences did not overlap were designated as secondary targets.

After Cynthia and Alex had determined their primary and secondary prospect categories, they were able to establish a set of criteria for each. Like housing developers, financial institutions became a primary target. But in order to become a part of their prospect list, a bank or savings and loan had to have several branch locations and a potential for growth. While Alex could handle public relations for a financial institution regardless of the number of branches, the criterion for multiple branches became important in order for them to pitch jointly, since Cynthia's focus would include creating special promotional events to launch new branches as the institution expanded.

In addition, Cynthia and Alex both prefer to work within two hours driving distance of their home office in order to be with their children each night. So all prospect businesses had to be within a one hundred mile radius of their home.

Cynthia and Alex began researching their prospect lists at their local library. The public library is a tremendous, often overlooked source of business information. The reference section contains a multitude of publications listing businesses by industry, size, and often by state and municipality. General business publications in many metropolitan areas regularly run lists by industry of the largest local companies. Trade publications are another source of vital information. They abound in a wide variety of industries and often publish annual directory issues with comprehensive national lists. Consult sources such as *Standard Rates and Data for Business Publications* to find trade publications listed by category and the *Gale Directory* for publications listed by locale.

Cynthia and Alex, for example, obtained a large list of the major financial institutions in their geographic market area from a local weekly business newspaper. They obtained a list of the major shopping mall management companies from a national trade publication by simply calling the publication and requesting a copy of the issue in which the listings, or rankings, had appeared. They then reviewed the list and culled all those headquartered in their area. After just a few short weeks, Cynthia and Alex had a comprehensive list of half a dozen categories with approximately ten prospect companies in each which met all of their personal criteria.

Once your prospect list has been compiled in virtually final form, all you will need are contact names. Simply review your industry categories and the prospect lists you have developed through preliminary research. For each category, determine the titles of the individuals within each organization who will be most capable of making a buying decision and/or be receptive to your sales message.

It's best to start as close to the top as possible. For example, Cynthia and Alex chose to pursue vice presidents of marketing in the financial category as the individuals most capable of making a senior-level decision concerning their public relations services.

Once you have determined the titles of those individuals to be contacted, gathering prospect names becomes as easy as calling and asking. Generally, receptionists will be helpful when asked, "We'd like to send some literature to your vice president of marketing. Can you tell me who to send it to?"

Where To Find Business-to-Business Leads

Your prospect lists, and even the categories you choose to pursue, will be in a continuing state of flux. As the economy, the market, and the types of services or products you offer evolve over time, you may wish to add new categories and drop others. As you work your prospect lists, unresponsive prospects or those you cannot convert will have to be replaced. And regular list maintenance and "cleaning"—after any direct mailing or at least several times per year—will shrink your lists due to address changes, business closings, job changes, and so forth.

Leads are everywhere. They're on television, on the radio, in newspaper articles and ads, in industry or trade articles, and in new product literature. You may even pick up leads from talks with friends and neighbors. When adding new leads or prospect companies to your lists, be certain to evaluate them and determine whether they meet all your initial criteria. And bear in mind that you cannot fully qualify a prospect until you begin the selling process.

Of course, the types of leads you gather will depend upon the nature of your business and your prospect categories, but it will help to get into the habit of keeping a pair of scissors handy while reading the newspaper, trade publications, business magazines, and other sources of information on prospects. Keep a pen and paper handy to jot down leads when watching television or when listening to the radio in the car. (Please pull over or wait until the next stop light to write them down!) You'll soon have a bulging file of prospect names which can then be evaluated and the qualified few added to your prospect lists.

Even if you are just starting your home-based business, you will have a variety of contacts and possibly a network of previously established prospects. Remember to add these to the lists. Once you have a combined list of prospects from research, new leads, and existing contacts, you are ready to refine your prospect list and begin working from it.

Just as you have been careful to gather leads from a wide range of sources, you should keep an eye open for any information concerning companies on your prospect list. Before contacting prospects, it's essential to know enough about them to determine what their needs might be and how your product or service will fill those needs. It's often helpful to develop dossiers on prospects which include the names of the key contacts (generally more than one), business and industry articles, and any miscellaneous information such as annual reports for public companies, sample ads, competitive information, and the like.

But beware: Never get bogged down in a lengthy information-gathering process at the expense of maintaining a proactive sales program. Why spend four or five hours over a month's time gathering page after page of information on a prospect when you may be rejected at the initial contact? Gather just enough information to be effective, to know whom you're talking to and what she or he might need from you. Too much information gathering can only slow you down.

Six Steps to Prospect List Development

Follow this six-point checklist to build your own comprehensive business-to-business prospect lists.

1. Narrow the target audience. Have you identified your audience by industry or profession? Where are they located geographically? What other criteria are important to you?

2. Use simple research. Have you visited the library to use national directories? Have you researched trade publications for lists in vertical industries? Have you explored lists available through other publications such as business or major metropolitan newspapers? If your target audience consists of members of any national, regional, or local associations, can you obtain membership lists?

3. Compile raw lists. Using the data available to you, have you eliminated those companies which do not fit your basic criteria?

4. Identify decision makers. Think about those individuals who are most capable of making a buying decision. What are their titles? When gathering names by telephone, have you checked carefully for spelling?

5. Add new leads over time. Are you practiced at gathering leads from media, friends, and other sources? Is each new lead evaluated by your original criteria?

6. Clean and update lists. Do you periodically review your lists to keep them current? If you use your lists for direct mail, frequent updating for address and personnel changes will reduce mailing costs by cutting down on undeliverables.

Four Essential Components of a Successful Sales Program

You've created comprehensive prospect lists and are ready to develop a proactive new business program which you can consistently manage throughout the year. It involves just four simple steps:

- making contacts
- tracking prospect information
- persistent, timely follow-up
- ongoing direct sales activity

For home-based entrepreneurs selling business products or services, the principal means for making contact with prospects is by telephone. Remember, you are working from your own prospect lists which have been narrowed to target qualified prospects in those business categories in which you have the greatest experience. You have the luxury of taking a personal approach—unlike consumer marketers who must reach thousands of prospects and thus rely on less personal means.

Set aside a regular time at least twice per week to make contact with prospects and to follow up with any necessary product or service literature. Until you have determined the best calling times for reaching your prospect groups, you may choose to set aside two or more hours one morning and again one afternoon per week, if you are already carrying a full business load. The less business you have in-house, the more time you may feel comfortable assigning to new business activities.

The time you have set aside will be reserved solely for making contacts and should not include any prospect meeting time or the hours involved in preparing proposals. Never let anything stand in the way of making regular contact with the prospects on your list. A dip in new business calls today may mean a dip in income later on.

Contact with prospects primarily includes cold calls to new prospects, or warm calls to those who have requested further information or who have come as referrals to you, and follow-up calls to prospects with whom you have previously spoken. For business-to-business sales, the goals of cold or warm calls are generally to qualify prospects, secure appointments, or raise prospect awareness prior to sending literature. Less often, when the product is a known, brand name and price is a key selling point, the goal of a cold call will be to complete a sale. Follow-up calls allow you to close for appointments or to settle on regular follow-up intervals for prospects who are further away from a buying decision.

Activities which tie in with marketing communications often must be included in the time set aside for making contact with prospects. The results of direct marketing, an essential tool for most business-to-business marketers, are greatly increased when small, manageable mailings are followed by telephone contact. As you schedule direct marketing activities for your company (see Chapter 8) be certain to schedule time to make these contacts along with your other prospect calls. Leads generated by advertising and public relations should also be followed up in the same manner.

Remember to be a good boss. Reward yourself when you make successful contacts with prospects and when hard work results in scheduled appointments or signed contracts. It's helpful to set goals which you can reasonably achieve. You may decide, for example, to set the goal of fifteen completed new business calls per week which result in two to three new business appointments. Susan B., who runs the wholesale distribution company mentioned in Chapter 1, likes to reward herself with a special dinner out at a fine restaurant for every three appointments she secures with prospects on her primary target list.

Tips for Making Prospect Follow-up and Tracking Easy

A sales tracking system is crucial to implementation of a successful new business program. Its most essential functions are to remind you of the dates on which prospect follow-up is indicated and the results of the last prospect contact, along with any other pertinent information. You may choose to use either a manual or computerized prospect tracking and tickler system. But whichever you prefer, the goal is to ensure consistent, timely follow-up.

Virtually all home-based businesses are run with the help of a computer. So if you are like most home-based business owners, chances are you will be maintaining your prospect and customer or client lists on disk. Nearly all word-processing programs provide some sort of mail merge capabilities for creating direct marketing letters, basic sales correspondence, lists, and labels. If your business has a limited client base and a small number of ongoing prospect companies—or if you don't use your computer daily—then a combination of word processing and a manual tickler system can serve you well.

A basic manual tickler system involves a call report, as in Figure 2.1, a three-ring binder, and a desk calendar. The results of every prospect contact are documented on a call report. The report itself will include any information which is pertinent to your type of business as well as basic prospect data: company name, address, telephone, contact names, size of company, competitive information. There will be space for pertinent notes made during the telephone call. And there is a final section for action to be taken; whether an appointment was scheduled, what literature was sent, and when you believe the prospect should be recontacted.

The call reports are then filed alphabetically in a handy three-ring binder and the date of the next follow-up is noted on your desk calendar. Pertinent prospect information gleaned from outside sources or during the lead gathering process may be clipped to the back of the call report and put in your binder. After an appointment is secured with a prospect, remove all her call reports from the binder and begin a prospect file.

Despite its simplicity, a manual tickler system becomes cumbersome when moderately large numbers of prospects are contacted regularly over a lengthy period of time. And it's hard to resist the many software programs which can manage both your sales and marketing communications systems at an extremely low cost. There are literally thousands of sales and account management software programs to choose from. Most, though not all, require a hard disk to run.

CALL REPORT

Telephone _____

Date _____   Category _____

Contact _____   Title _____

Company _____

Address _____

_____

Info: _____

_____

_____

_____

_____

_____

_____

_____

Planning: _____ annual _____ year-round _____ none

Implementation: _____ in-house _____ other

Action Taken: _____ Appt. _____ Date _____ Time

_____ Letter _____ Brochure _____ Other

Call Back: _____ 2 wks. _____ 1 mo. _____ 3 mo. _____ 6 mo.

Add to list: _____ Yes _____ No _____ Delete

Figure 2.1

An ideal system should perform tracking functions, maintain tickler files which retrieve leads by date of follow-up, file call reports to document contacts, and maintain lists. Many generate letters and labels as well.

Both *Sales and Marketing Management* and *Business Marketing* magazines publish comprehensive directories of sales and marketing communications software programs. Both of these sources plus *Home-Office Computing* provide excellent information to help you choose the right software for your home-based business. Some of the most highly rated programs sell for under five hundred dollars.

For Emanuel's translation/language services, a manual tickler system is adequate. With just four prospect categories and fewer than fifty primary prospects overall, he is quite capable of maintaining his system without the need for a computer software program specially designed for tracking and retrieval of leads. Emanuel is extremely well organized and careful to consult his calendar daily to prevent follow-up calls from falling through the cracks in his busy schedule.

Cynthia and Alex, on the other hand, could never function successfully without the help of a computer software program for sales and marketing communications. The sheer number of prospects they must reach in order to grow their public relations firm mandates the need for such software. Having the program also helps Alex know when it is time to prod Cynthia, who often falls behind in her prospect calls and follow-up.

The single most essential component of your manual or computerized prospect tracking system is consistent follow-up. In many industries, it may require months and often years to obtain appointments with key prospects and even longer to convert them into customers or clients. During that time, follow-up will generally take the form of call backs at predetermined intervals—for example, after two and six months, one year, or more frequently—depending upon the prospect's interest or buying cycles.

For business-to-business marketers, telephone contact may also be combined with direct marketing either as part of an ongoing marketing communications program or simply in the form of an individual sales letter sent to smooth the way for scheduled telephone follow-up. Your fax machine is also a handy tool for providing an essential "hook" for your follow-up telephone contact. Try faxing a trade magazine article on a topic of special interest to your prospect the day before your scheduled telephone follow up. This will both provide you with a "reason" for calling and your prospect with the motivation to take the call.

Consumer sales ────────────────────────────

How To Prospect Less and Sell More

If you are a home-based business owner marketing a consumer product or service, you are facing an entirely different set of prospecting challenges than your friends who are marketing to businesses. Unlike business marketers, who can create prospect lists through research, consumer marketers must generally rely on referrals and well-targeted marketing communications programs to generate leads or sales.

Faced with a vast number of potential buyers, target marketing strategies are crucial to producing a manageable and affordable new business program. Whether you are selling a consumer service or product, begin by identifying your geographic market area. Will it be local, regional, or national? Will it be focused on key urban areas or is your product geared toward rural audiences?

Then consider the demographic characteristics of your target audiences, such as age, sex, and income. Will you be selling to men or women? How old are they? Does their household income play a strong role in whether they can afford your product or service?

The more you know about your target audiences and their buying habits, the better you can fine-tune your sales and marketing communications programs. And well-targeted programs cost less to implement and will generally produce superior results.

Developing a Target Audience Profile for Your Consumer Service

Kathleen M. has been running a successful interior design business from her home for nearly two years. Kathleen's home itself is a showplace decorated so as to demonstrate her creative capabilities to friends and potential clients.

But starting a home-based business was never Kathleen's goal—that is, until she was suddenly laid off from the department store interior design group where she had worked successfully for nearly nine years. A pricey, well-known chain, Kathleen's employer was suffering from losses due to increased competition exacerbated by a dip in retail sales, and was forced to declare chapter eleven. While the stores remained open nationwide, severe cutbacks were undertaken and Kathleen's job was eliminated virtually overnight.

So, armed with years of experience, a Rolodex of contacts, and a good mental list of past, satisfied clients, Kathleen decided to give herself ninety days to test whether or not she could be successful at running her own business. In the past, Kathleen's clients had primarily been women who lived in the upper-middle-income suburbs surrounding the department store. In many cases, they and their families had recently purchased homes in the area—sometimes their second or third move within a ten- to fifteen-mile radius. Others were remodeling or redecorating their homes in lieu of moving. Her clients had ranged in age from their late twenties to about fifty. And none came from the extremely affluent neighborhoods where employing a"name" interior designer was considered imperative to one's social standing. By using her past client list to determine the profile of her initial, primary target audience, Kathleen could identify her prospective clients by geographic market area, age, sex, household income levels, and in some cases, length of residence. Thanks to this narrow focus and a lot of hard work, the results at the end of her three-month trial period were most encouraging. And today, Kathleen has a flourishing business.

For most consumer service businesses, sales are driven by marketing communications. Advertising, PR, sales promotion, direct marketing, and other communications tools all yield leads, effectively narrowing the infinite universe of potential consumers to a manageable stream of more qualified prospects which can be cultivated through one-on-one sales contact.

Consumer service businesses are extremely time intensive. Yet they must be consistently supported by sales activity as a follow-up to leads generated by ongoing marketing communications. To create a manageable program, the level of sales activities and marketing communications expenditures should be scaled according to your personal and business growth goals.

- Do you envision your company employing others? How many?

- Do you hope to move the business out of your home as it grows, or are you right where you want to stay?

- How many prospects/leads must you call on to gain one customer?

- How many customers do you need and want? How many can you effectively service?

The answers to these and other critical questions should become increasingly clear after your first few months of operation, although your business goals may continually evolve over time and in response to competitive and market changes. If your present goals include exponential growth for your home-based business, you must staff for ongoing sales and budget marketing communications accordingly. When developing your target audience profile consider:

Most consumer service businesses are limited/focused by the geographic market area they can serve. Will driving 180 miles (two hours each way) to visit a prospective client be as lucrative as visiting two clients during that same period of time closer to home?

Other consumer service businesses, such as childcare or home health care for the elderly, are more influenced by target audience age—targeting parents of young children or adult children of aging parents, for example.

Some, like interior designers and remodeling contractors, use household income as a critical determinant of prospect status. Your best prospect is always one you know can afford to make a buying decision.

While few consumer service businesses are marketed to either one sex or the other, determining whether your primary target audience will be males, females, or both—and in what proportion—may be critical to the success of your new business program. It is not uncommon to sell the same consumer service to both men and women using a different set of benefits and sales tactics due to the differences between what men and women want to buy.

Once you have determined your geographic market area and the demographic profile of your primary target audience, you are ready to develop a new business program.

Four-Step Prospecting Program for Consumer Services

New business prospecting activities for your consumer service company will include four basic steps:

- handling incoming leads
- recording and tracking prospect names
- telephone follow-up/warm calls
- proactive direct sales activity

Prospect calls (leads) from marketing communications will be coming in all the time. It will be essential to take these calls or be as available as possible. Potential customers or clients will make instantaneous judgments concerning the quality and responsiveness of your service business based on the first few seconds of telephone contact with your company.

Most consumers, particularly those seeking costly services such as home remodeling or interior design, may be put off by answering machine messages in general and will always respond negatively to a message which sounds too personal, unbusinesslike, or in any way unprofessional. You may wish to have telephone backup during your busiest times of the day or week, or engage a competent answering service if you receive a large number of high-end consumer calls. If your target audience is such that prospects are not put off by answering machine messages, then consider having your answering machine or voice mail message recorded by a "professional secretary soundalike."

Once you retrieve your messages from a service or answering machine, it is imperative to return all calls, if not the same day, certainly as quickly as possible. Countless business dollars are lost daily by consumer service companies through failure to demonstrate responsiveness to prospective customers. Fine-tuning your sales and marketing communications programs and professional support requirements may take time, but remember—if you are too busy doing the day-to-day work to return or take new business calls, you are missing opportunities to grow your business. Depending upon the message in the marketing communications vehicle which generates the leads, your incoming calls may result in a request for information or brochure, a price quote, or even an appointment. This first contact presents your initial opportunity to qualify prospects and lay the groundwork for future follow-up.

Ron G. has been operating a custom home remodeling business for nearly ten years. He employs a crew of six and is out of his home office virtually 90 percent of the time, either calling on prospective clients or working on remodeling jobs. Ron uses marketing communications and referrals to gain the majority of his new business leads. Newspaper and magazine ads along with direct mail to well-targeted lists yield a steady stream of incoming calls which are deftly fielded by Ron's office manager, Lee.

Lee's job is to make certain each incoming prospect caller is qualified prior to setting up an appointment for Ron to visit his/her home and bid on a remodeling project. Even if the prospective client is merely shopping for further information, such as a brochure on Ron's custom remodeling business, Lee makes certain to complete a lead report, such as the one shown in Fugure 2.2.

In addition to the basic data—name, address and telephone number—she determines the type of remodeling the prospect is considering, his time frame for the work, and anticipated budget. Finally, Lee inquires how the customer learned about Ron's remodeling and records that information on the lead report for later use in assessing the effectiveness of ongoing marketing communications activities.

Qualifying and recording incoming leads is a vital step in establishing a new business program. Lead reports will not only fill the need for immediate information but will also help you determine over time the source of your best pros-

---

LEAD REPORT

Date: _____

Time: _____

Name: _____

Telephone: (day) _____   (evening) _____

Address: _____

_____

Type of project: _____

_____

_____

Budget: _____

Prospect request: Information _____ Estimate _____

Lead source: Referral _____ Saw ad in _____

Direct mail _____ Other _____

Follow up date: _____

Figure 2.2

pects. They will reveal the times of day, week, month, or year your greatest number of leads are likely to be generated, and by which sources. They will assist you in refining a target audience profile based on those prospects which convert to customers. In short, ongoing scrutiny and analysis of leads generated provides information essential to fine-tuning programs and budgets.

Each day, Lee inputs the information from the lead reports into their sales and marketing database. Once Ron has met with a prospective customer, the information on the results of that meeting are added to the prospect files along with a date notation for telephone follow-up. Plus, each week Lee prints out a list by date of all prospects who have simply requested further information. These prospects require follow-up (warm calls), and Ron sets aside at least several hours per week just for this activity.

The quantity of incoming leads necessary to sustain consumer service businesses like Ron G.'s make manual tickler and tracking systems too cumbersome and inefficient. Fortunately, the abundance of sales and other software available—many programs selling for under five hundred dollars—makes running even a large new business program manageable for the home-based business owner.

The best programs make recording and managing data easy. They provide forms to record prospect information, maintain tickler files which retrieve leads by date of follow-up, perform tracking functions, file reports to document contacts, maintain lists for marketing communications, offer sample letters, and generate labels.

Sales and Marketing Management and *Business Marketing* magazines publish comprehensive directories of such software. *Home-Office Computing* provides regular reviews of a wide range of contact management programs for both Mac and DOS users. They have evaluated most of the popular programs and would be a good source of information for any home-based business owner in search of the right software to meet the needs of a growing business.

Virtually all qualified prospects require personal follow-up. This is particularly true in service businesses where the prospects' estimation of your ability to perform may chiefly determine whether you are awarded the job.

For consumer service business owners, warm calls are generally the preferred method of follow-up to prospects who have requested and received further information or literature. When incoming prospect calls have generated appointments or bids, follow-up calls are the essential next step to move prospects closer to a buying decision.

Be certain to set aside regular days and times for telephone follow-up to prospects with whom you have already met and warm calls to those who have received your literature. It may be necessary to allocate evening hours several times a week for these activities if the bulk of your consumer prospects work during the daytime.

While many of your prospects will have no qualms about discussing personal services during business hours, others may. In this situation it is best to ask each prospect at what time in the evening he or she would like to be recontacted, and follow suit. In this way, your evening call becomes a thoughtfully scheduled appointment, not an intrusion.

But whether you restrict yourself to day or evening calls or a combination of both, the time you set aside for telephone follow-up must be separate from the hours scheduled for preparing proposals or bids and attending new business meetings. Whether to gain an appointment or ask again for the business, consistent, timely follow-up is essential to new business success. So be certain to stay current and never let these important activities fall by the wayside.

How To Target Prospects for Consumer Products

When selling a consumer product, particularly if you have your eye on national sales, you may wish to consider more than demographic and geographic criteria when developing a target audience profile. Many consumer marketers look at the geodemographic makeup of their target audiences as well.

Geodemography (segmenting the population based on the tendency of people to live in neighborhoods with others like themselves) groups people into types or clusters based on their lifestyles. Individuals or households belonging to one group may tend to buy trend-setting products while members of another group or cluster are expected to spend more conservatively. Geodemographic information helps marketers to identify and locate their most likely buyers.

To sell a product to a narrow audience, even on a market-by-market basis, direct mail lists are often subjected to cluster analysis. In other words, the lists are analyzed, sometimes by zip code or census track, to determine which individuals fall into the clusters most likely to provide customers. In effect, geodemography is simply another means of segmenting the wide universe of potential consumers by narrowing it down to include only those groups which are most likely to buy a given product. This is of particular relevance to catalogue marketers, whose goal must always be to mail the fewest number of catalogues possible to generate their required sales volume.

For specific information on how you can use geodemography to market your consumer product, you may wish to contact one of the three large firms which license mailing list houses to encode residential mailing lists by cluster. They are Claritas, CACI, Inc., and Donnelly Marketing.

Creating an Affordable Program for Your Consumer Product

Like consumer services, sales of consumer products will be driven by marketing communications. To many home-based entrepreneurs, launching a marketing communications campaign on a national level, for example, might at first appear unthinkable. Yet by narrowly defining your target audience, no matter what the size of the geographic market area, marketing communications costs may be significantly streamlined.

For example, while many types of consumers may wish to buy mail order herbs, a narrower profile may show the mail order herb buyer to be an affluent, well-educated, and risk-oriented urbanite, who enjoys cooking and entertaining at home. This would dramatically narrow the field of potential advertising vehicles to just a few, such as *Gourmet* and *New York* magazines, while at the same time permitting an affordable, national campaign to generate the highest number of qualified buyers.

But whether local, regional, or national, your lead generation campaign must yield buyers and—to be profitable—a low percentage of unqualified information seekers. Use of an 800 number will stimulate credit card orders and can be easily and affordably arranged with your long-distance carrier.

Unlike consumer service businesses, consumer product sales yield the largest number of incoming calls. Ideally, the greatest number are orders, followed by customer service calls and returns. Depending upon your geographic market area, the size and success of your marketing communications activities, and your in-house support, you may wish to contract with an outside service for handling incoming calls and compilation and maintenance of your customer database.

Ginnie and Sam P. run a successful nursery business specializing in hard-to-find herbs. When they began, their business consisted primarily of sales to local customers, friends and neighbors who would visit the greenhouse located on their small farm. To grow the business, they decided to place a series of small, classified mail order ads in just one national publication which they believed targeted their most likely buyers.

Over time, and with the addition of an 800 number to the ads, orders began to increase. It became clear, if Ginnie and Sam were to continue to enjoy growing their fine herbs as well as their business, that order processing and database management would have to be handled by a qualified service bureau—one that would take the care with customers for which Ginnie and Sam were well known. At present, they are pleased with the growth of their small, home-based business, and development of a national catalogue for mailing to their customer base may well be in their future.

While this book is not meant as a guide for developing a mail order or catalogue company, you may wish to consider that as one effective means of increasing sales for your consumer product business.

Although some consumer products—everything from pottery to bird feeders, to glass paperweights—may be sold exclusively through marketing communications and by word-of-mouth, many unique or luxury items sell best when the customer has the opportunity to see, touch, and in some way experience them. For these products, some retail exposure is essential to increasing sales. Often, creating a sales program to grow a consumer product business must include a combination of business-to-business sales strategies combined with a marketing/communications-driven consumer sales program.

If you recall from the example of Judy's jewelry in Chapter 1, sales of her costly creations remained confined to a small circle of customers until she expanded her sales strategies to include direct sales to retail stores which would carry her line. By convincing retail stores or businesses to display and sell your products, you essentially obtain a wide salesforce and the opportunity to exponentially increase your company's sales.

So, to expand sales of your consumer product business, consider:

- using well-targeted marketing communications to drive sales
- developing a business-to-business sales strategy, securing others to sell your product for you.

There are many instances in which both methods might be employed to create an effective, ongoing sales program. Leisha E.'s business is a perfect example. When pregnant with her first child, Leisha simply could not find a comfortable position in which to sleep at night. And along with the birth of her child came the birth of a successful business idea—creation of a maternity pillow which would make comfortable sleep possible during pregnancy.

Leisha formed a partnership with her good friend, a dressmaker, and they were soon producing maternity pillows for their wide circle of friends. PR coverage from a local newspaper spread word of their product throughout the community, and orders expanded. Orders increased further when Leisha began a well-targeted, small-space advertising campaign in carefully selected national publications. A local factory was soon engaged to manufacture the maternity pillows, and a small in-house staff of two handled incoming telephone and mail-order processing.

As demand for the product grew and Leisha was able to demonstrate a track record for successful sales, she began a full-scale business-to-business sales effort targeting local retailers—complete with a well-crafted presentation to illustrate the benefits a retailer would derive by carrying her maternity pillows and other related products. Within several years, an idea which had been born out of discomfort was making pregnant women comfortable all across America.

Putting Your Sales Program into Action

As a home-based entrepreneur, your business's single greatest asset is YOU. Your knowledge, experience, expertise, devotion to quality work, and superior customer service—in effect, all the special characteristics you possess—will make your business uniquely yours and unlike any other. It's no wonder many new business owners take negative sales results, minor defeats, and setbacks more personally than they ever did when working for someone else or as part of a larger corporate structure.

People hire people, not companies. And they hire people they like, trust, and believe are, in some measure, like themselves. That's why creating prospect lists, generating, tracking, and following up leads are only half the story when it comes to developing a proactive sales program. The second half involves building interpersonal relationships with prospects along with a solid reputation.

For both business-to-business and consumer sales, it's essential to be proactive. Engage in activities which bring you into one-on-one contact with members of your target groups. A vital component of Leisha E.'s strategy to expand sales of her maternity pillows and related items includes attending and displaying at national trade shows where she can meet with and get to know chain store buyers.

Alex S. is growing the public relations practice he shares with his wife, Cynthia, through a carefully structured program of sales activities. Alex has become a member and regularly attends meetings of professional associations or clubs whose memberships are comprised of his target prospect groups—bankers and real estate developers. By attending these meetings, workshops, and luncheons, Alex has, over time, been developing relationships with key individuals whose names have been added to his company's database for follow-up along with other prospects.

In addition to merely attending meetings of his target prospect groups, Alex offers himself as a speaker on public relations topics of special interest to these audiences. As a result, when making his follow-up calls to prospects he has met in this manner, he is more than just another public relations executive selling his services. He is a business associate and recognized "expert."

Alex also writes and submits articles to trade publications read by his target audiences. These articles enhance his image as an expert or guru, give his joint PR practice credibility, and greatly improve the results from his new business prospecting calls.

Kathleen M. knows that length of residence—under six months—is an important characteristic of prospects most in need of her interior design services. Her marketing communications activities include direct mail to lists of new movers, ads featuring a new neighbor discount, and sales literature enclosed in all welcome wagon packages. In conjunction with these lead producers, Kathleen's direct sales program targeting new movers includes closely tracking real estate closings (homes sold) in her primary geographic market area through Realtor newsletters, the local newspaper, and "Sold" signs on the homes themselves. Within approximately thirty days of the new homeowners' arrival, Kathleen personally stops by to greet them and drop off her literature.

After lengthy negotiation and a lot of hard work, Kathleen was also able to convince the builder of a new home subdivision in her geographic market area to offer a discount on her interior design services to all new homebuyers as an incentive. In exchange for free interior design of the builder's model homes, Kathleen secured the opportunity to display her creative capabilities and sell her services to the majority of new homeowners.

In addition to new homeowners like these, many of Kathleen's best clients are simply redecorating older homes. So her proactive sales program also includes participation in local civic organizations where she interacts regularly in a more social setting with members of her target prospect group. As a result, she has raised awareness of her services within her target group and paved the way for future business.

Ron G. considers his past remodeling clients his best salespeople and makes a point of continually asking for referrals. At the finish of each remodeling project, Ron's clients receive an evaluation sheet on which they are asked to record their impressions of the job and the way the work was performed. At the bottom of the sheet is a request for the names of two referrals—friends or associates who the client believes would like to learn more about Ron's home remodeling services. Thanks to the superior quality of his team's work, the majority of Ron's clients are happy to provide referrals.

How To Plan Sales Strategy and Long-Range Tactics

When formulating your own proactive sales program, remember to keep it manageable. Plan for activities that will produce both immediate and long-term results.

Strategic thinking comes first. Make a list of all activities you believe will bring you in contact with those prospects who are closest to making a buying decision. Consider the tactics—or actual methodology—for each of your strategies. Can you reasonably expect to carry on these activities consistently and with enough care so as to profit from them? Are the strategies consistent with the image of your company? For example, soliciting overseas visitors arriving at airline terminals might be a great way to sell today's tour, but will it build your sightseeing tour business over time, create an appropriate image for your firm among other tour operators—and is it legal?

Narrow the list down to activities which you can consistently carry out in conjunction with the day-to-day demands of your growing business. These activities will take precedence over others which simply lay the groundwork for future sales, such as participation in civic or professional associations. Finally, add to your list only those relationship-building activities which you can handle without jeopardizing your ability to perform your list of more direct sales tactics.

Your short list of proactive sales strategies and the tactics or methodologies you will use to employ them should be formalized and have performance dates assigned. In essence, you will formulate *what* you are going to do—the strategies—and *how* you are going to do it—the tactics. Then, such factors as *when*—the actual dates scheduled—and the ways these activities will be tied into or dependent upon marketing communications tools and programs should be considered.

Even before creating an ongoing marketing communications program for your home-based business (as outlined in Chapter 8) consider how the budget for support materials and other tools will impact the feasibility of your sales strategies.

For example, you are a real estate sales associate and your strategy involves meeting homeowners and introducing them to your service through sales literature. The tactics employed will require going door-to-door, shaking hands and distributing literature. But no marketing communications budget exists for producing quality literature in sufficient quantities. So your strategy will have to be modified or the tactic eliminated. It's better to come up with another tactic or a larger budget than to pass out shoddy looking flyers which will denigrate the perceived quality of your services.

Targeting Current Customers and Clients for Repeat Sales

When building your ongoing sales program, it is important to include past and current customers or clients in your plans. It's always less costly to resell an old client than to win a new one. Indeed, every sale lays the groundwork for the next.

Do you remember these words from the old song we learned as children, "Make new friends and keep the old. One is silver and the other gold"? This is essentially true when it comes to business. Consider how many of the nation's largest companies have been built on the strength of customer loyalty and repeat sales.

To consistently grow your business over time, always maintain a database or complete list of customers or clients and address them through a combination of marketing communications and sales activities. Never assume, because a customer or client has not openly voiced dissatisfaction with your product or service in the past, that he or she will automatically reorder or renew. Numerous studies have shown that Americans, when dissatisfied, are unlikely to complain. Only a small percentage ever voice their displeasure in letters or telephone calls. Happy, satisfied customers are themselves continually bombarded by competing sales messages, constantly being tempted to try something "new." So be sure to ask for the business again and again to build repeat sales and relationships that are golden.

chapter three

Expert Tips for Using the Telephone Like a Pro

Richard H. didn't believe in cold calling. After all, he had spent over twenty years in association management. He'd founded his association management company to provide high-quality, professional guidance to small associations in need of his senior-level expertise, not to become "just some salesman."

Richard opened his business with one client in hand. Another soon followed, thanks to his many contacts and business associates. To gain additional business, Richard created a #10 size brochure which he mailed to a small list of potential clients. He personally informed all his principal contacts of his new company, and he continued to attend the monthly meetings of the professional association to which he belonged—where he proudly passed out new business cards.

When Richard received three or four responses to his mailing, he took care to meet quickly with each prospect over lunch at a fine restaurant. But he never initiated telephone calls to any of the prospects on his mailing list. When his business did not grow further during the first eight months, Richard sent a letter to his mailing list. Then another on his company's one year anniversary.

Within eighteen months of having started his business, Richard saw the departure of one of his two clients. His business wasn't growing. It was shrinking. He began to dream up all manner of reasons for his lack of success— "Surely the market is wrong... Prospects are simply too dull to see the value of my services... My brochure doesn't carry the right messages... If only friends and associates would send business instead of just letting me down...." In just a little over two years from the time he started his home-based business, Richard was once again someone else's employee.

Richard's story is all too familiar. Like many other intelligent, successful individuals he had failed to learn an important lesson when he made the change from employee to business owner: *To get the business you desire, you must be willing to ask for it. And ask the right people, the right way.*

The telephone is an essential and irreplaceable tool for growing any business. For home-based business owners, use of the telephone takes on even greater importance since the trade-offs for privacy, freedom, and an improved lifestyle are often lack of company visibility and personal isolation. Yet many small businesses quietly close within the first several years of operation after turnover of their initial customers or accounts. This is due, at least in part, to their owners' lack of telephone selling skills or disproportionate fear of being rejected by a voice on the other end of the line.

This chapter contains all the fundamentals you'll need to initiate productive contact with prospects and to follow up leads generated by marketing communications. With practice and mastery of these few simple techniques, you will soon be asking for—and winning—business your company can rely on for sustained growth.

Overcoming Fear with Consultative Selling

One of the most challenging and fascinating aspects of cold or warm calling is that you, not the prospects, determine your own success or failure. You are in control, and your own self-image, knowledge, and expertise will either make you successful or doom you to failure.

There are two things which can condemn anyone, beginner or expert, to failure right from the start: fear and a negative self-image. The thought of selling is intimidating to many people. Cold or warm calling may be new to you, and it is only natural to be uncertain about how you will be received by prospects. Even if you are trained and experienced in sales, once you begin selling your own company, the picture changes. Now, you are largely selling yourself and a business or concept which is your own personal creation. Emotionally, you feel at greater personal risk, and you may tend to take even minor rejection personally.

On the other hand, there is tremendous satisfaction to be gained by helping a prospect to experience the benefits of your product or service in a way that meets his or her needs. Insecurity (and consequently, call reluctance) stems from fear, the fear of being personally rejected. Satisfaction comes from uncovering and filling needs in a friendly, noncombative, and supportive way. This is called *consultative selling*.

How To Project a Positive Self-Image

Think of the prospects with whom you speak, even for the first time, as if they were your best friends looking to you for advice. Use the same relaxed tone and enthusiastic manner. New business owners and entrepreneurs are great risk takers because they have learned to adapt to risk and take it in stride. But if the challenges you face in cold or warm calling begin to appear intimidating or overwhelming, consider: When you take risks in selling, do you need more approval than reality suggests? Are you expecting an unfriendly reaction? How do you perceive normal skepticism?

When you imagine the prospect on the other end of the line as a friend or associate looking to you for advice, you can effectively throw away the old, negative images you may have been conjuring up. Ask yourself, What is the very worst that could happen? The friend—your prospect—might choose not to take your advice. But you will have created a positive and potentially lasting impression before moving on to the next prospect on your list.

Compose a positive affirmation, and if you are still uneasy, write it down and keep it in front of you as you make your calls. A good positive affirmation for someone practicing consultative selling—uncovering and filling prospect needs based on supportive interaction—is, "I am a confident, competent professional here to help."

Next, think about what you will help your clients or customers achieve. Compose a *mission statement* which defines your purpose. Begin with, "My purpose is to help my clients/customers," and end with the benefits they will derive. You can write this mission statement down or simply think about it as you begin to make your new business calls. Here are some examples.

RON G.'S CUSTOM HOME REMODELING:

"My purpose is to help my clients obtain top quality remodeling work completed on time and within the agreed upon budget."

CYNTHIA AND ALEX S.'S PUBLIC RELATIONS COMPANY:

"Our purpose is to help our clients raise awareness and enhance their companys' images through consistent, well-targeted placements of appropriate editorial."

SUSAN B.'S WHOLESALE DISTRIBUTION BUSINESS:

"My purpose is to help my clients receive the best prices on name brands and timely delivery on every order."

When you present the self-image of a positive professional out to perform a service or offer a product which will benefit those with whom you interact, you will be more concerned with how much prospects need your expertise.

After all, you are a confident, competent professional here to help each customer or prospect achieve his or her goals.

Enthusiasm and Ego: Two Essential Ingredients

There is a certain excitement inherent in starting and running your own business. This excitement, this enthusiasm, is contagious, particularly when coupled with success stories.

Consider what you have done to solve problems or meet special challenges for customers or clients and be prepared to discuss two or three *case histories.* It's not important whether these accomplishments took place while you were working for someone else or on your own. It matters only that you concentrate on the ways in which you have helped customers meet their goals. Then your natural enthusiasm will make you want to tell prospects about all the wonderful things you can do for them.

There is no one alive who is able to convert every prospect every time. Professional salespeople understand this and accept occasional defeat as a part of normal day-to-day life—and so must you. The ability to pick up and go on without dwelling on "the one that got away" is called *ego strength.* It's what will carry you through every day with a positive and supportive attitude—eschewing rejection and refusing to take minor setbacks personally.

Ego drive is what pushes you on to look for the next prospect and better ways of meeting that prospect's goals. Chances are, the more successful you are as a business owner or entrepreneur, the more likely you are to be strong and highly positive that what you do is important and needed day in and day out.

Because you are constantly looking for better ways of doing things, you see yourself as competent, knowledgeable, and expert. And that comes across to prospects whether in

cold calling or handling incoming calls. Once you have overcome your fears and have a positive self-image, you will be able
to relax because you will have discovered the worst possible
thing that could happen to you really isn't much at all.

Ask Yourself, What Do They Need From Me?

In Chapter 1, you created a solid sales and marketing communications platform based on the benefits your prospects
can expect to derive from your product or service. Before
making any prospect call, ask yourself, "What does he need
from me?" By assessing a prospect's needs before ever picking up the telephone, you can mentally arrange your key
selling points in such a way that they create appropriate
expectations based on what you believe he wants to buy.
Once your prospect's needs are determined, the ways you
can fill them should become relatively clear.

Following the guidelines in Chapter 2, you have formu-
lated lists of qualified prospects, initiated a marketing communications campaign which has generated leads, or both.
Your next step is to cultivate essential skills which will assist
you when initiating or answering prospect calls.

Setting Realistic and Achievable Call Objectives: Three Examples

For most businesspeople, the objective of a cold call is rarely
to close a sale. Instead, cold call objectives may range from
qualifying prospects, providing price quotes, gaining appointments, or any number of initiating steps which pave the
way for future sales. Warm calling—initiating contact with
prospects who have expressed interest in your product or
service—may likewise entail a range of objectives depending
upon the nature of your business.

The objectives you set for cold or warm calling must be realistic and achievable yet move the prospect incrementally closer to a buying decision.

EXAMPLE 1. Cynthia and Alex S., public relations practitioners, are selling their professional services to local businesses. The objective of their cold calls is always to close for an appointment. For them, the cold call is the first step in a lengthy selling process which includes an initial cold call and possibly two or three follow-up calls until an appointment is secured, prospect meetings and interviews, preparation and presentation of a proposal, presentation of a contract, and closing.

EXAMPLE 2. Susan B. is a wholesale distributor selling industrial products to businesses nationwide. As she cannot meet personally with each and every prospect, her cold calling objective is to qualify the prospect and gain enough information to produce a quote for supplying products from one of her many lines. Additionally, Susan will always set a date for follow-up after the prospect has received her quote, so that she can close the sale by telephone.

While Susan cannot meet with every prospect nationwide, she does visit with her principal clients in key cities and towns within a two- to three-month cycle. And when cold calling, Susan's objective may change to include closing for an appointment with a major prospect in a city she plans to visit in the near future.

EXAMPLE 3. Ron G., who offers custom home remodeling services to local consumers, uses warm calls to follow up leads generated by marketing communications. Ron's office manager, Lee, has pre-qualified prospects to a limited extent and, in some cases, has supplied them with company literature. So Ron's warm call objective is to qualify further and close for an appointment. If a viable prospect isn't ready or willing to meet, Ron will close for the best date and time for future follow up.

You will note that in all three examples the goal of a cold or warm call is to move the prospect significantly closer to a purchase. A secondary or weaker objective, such as simply sending literature which informs the prospect, is used only in those cases where the primary objective cannot be met. As you make your call, focus on your objective without being overanxious, and never lose sight of it as you guide the interaction to its logical conclusion.

The Secret of Effective Openers

You are completely prepared with a good mental attitude, you are aware of whom you are calling and what he or she might need from you. You've set a call objective which will move your prospect along the path to a buying decision. And now you are ready to pick up the phone and make your first cold call.

Many business owners find the opening statement the most difficult part of a call. It will help if you understand that people do things for their own reasons and not yours—they want to know what's in it for them. Therefore, an effective opening statement must always include some introduction of yourself and your company followed by an opening benefit.

Use your sales platform to develop an opening benefit which is of particular relevance to your prospects. Avoid inner-directed openers. These are "I" openers such as:

"Could I have a few minutes of your time?"

"I just wanted to call and tell you a little bit about my company."

"I was wondering if you might be interested in..."

Prospects don't care what you want, but only what is going to meet their special needs. Here are several examples of solid openers which include an introduction and a benefit.

"Hello. This is Alex Smith of Cynthia and Alex's public relations company. [Pause for acknowledgment.] We're a full service PR company specializing in working with financial institutions like yours. My special reason for calling today is to see if we may share with you several ideas we have which will enhance the image of your bank and increase customer traffic on the branch level."

"Hello. This is Ron Gomez of Ron's custom home remodeling. [Pause for acknowledgment.] Thank you for your recent interest in working with my firm. Our clients who've chosen the kind of quality sunroom addition you're considering have found it not only becomes their favorite room but also really adds to the potential resale value of their homes."

"This is Susan Bower of Susan's wholesale distribution corporation. [Pause for acknowledgment.] We're one of the country's fastest growing wholesale distributors of industrial rubber flooring. My special reason for calling is to tell you about the new low pricing structure we've set up for companies like yours which are large purchasers of XYZ flooring."

Spend some time writing down a few openers and then try them out. But once you've practiced them several times, be sure to throw away your script. Never read from a canned speech, even if it's just a few sentences. Such an impersonal approach is insulting to prospects and counter to the goal of consultative selling: to meet the unique needs of each individual prospect.

How To Ask Questions That Qualify Prospects

By addressing a benefit specific to the prospect's needs, the last section of the opener paves the way for you to begin qualifying. Following the opener you may ask, "Did I catch you at a good time?" This further demonstrates your caring attitude and a desire to meet the prospect's needs. Virtually all prospects will respond with the equivalent of, "It's never a good time, but go ahead." This isn't surprising as a telephone call is by and large an unscheduled interruption. The way you frame your call and the opening benefit you use will determine whether your interruption is, indeed, a welcome one.

In order to qualify prospects, you must do two things effectively:

- ask pertinent questions
- listen to the answers

There are two types of questions. *Closed end questions* are those which can be answered yes or no. These are fact finding questions. We use closed end questions because we need facts. They are good ice breakers. They gain attention. They can draw out a silent person. They can elicit the preferred answer. They can change direction, qualify a point, make a point or pinpoint a specific need. On the telephone, as in much of our normal conversation, we do a lot with closed end questions.

Open end questions ask, "What do you feel about X?" They are feeling/finding questions. Open end questions are used to gather general information and, most important, to uncover emotional background. You should use these questions as long as the prospect is willing.

In other words, closed end questions are conversation starters. Open end questions allow you to qualify the prospect carefully and assess all of his needs and desires.

Examples of closed end questions are, "How long have you been using your present supplier?" or "What is your current public relations budget?" Examples of open end questions are, "What do you like best about your present supplier?" or "How do you feel about the results you're getting in proportion to your public relations expenditures?"

Asking questions is essential to gaining information and building rapport. So in order to be effective on the telephone you must use a combination of open and closed end questions well. The following quick exercises will help you develop the simple skills necessary. Remember, closed end questions reveal facts. Open end questions reveal underlying background and emotions.

Exercise 1: Closed End Questions

On a blank sheet of paper, make a list of all the closed end questions you might ask a prospect in the course of a normal telephone conversation. Skip two or three lines between each question (You'll need this space for the next exercise).

The following is a sample list of closed end questions Susan B. might use with a prospect for her wholesale distribution company:

Who is your present supplier?

How long have you been working with them?

What is your order volume per year?

How long have you been with the company?

Are you the person responsible for placing orders?

How often do you order?

At what times of the year do you order?

What types of products do you order?

Do you meet regularly with your suppliers?

Do they offer volume discounts?

Do they deliver in 48 hours or less?

Do your orders ever arrive late or damaged?

What percentage of the time?

Do your present suppliers assign one individual rep to handle all your needs?

Are you happy with your present suppliers?

Exercise 2: Open End Questions

On the same sheet of paper, rephrase each closed end question as an open end question. Write down only the types of questions you might use to qualify one of your own prospects on the telephone.

The following examples are for Susan B.'s wholesale distribution company:

Who is your present supplier?
How did you choose your present supplier?

How long have you been working with them?
How important is it to maintain long standing relationships with your suppliers?

What is your order volume per year?
Why do you think your order volume will go up this year?

How long have you been with the company?
What are the special qualities of ABC company that have kept you happy there for so long?

Are you the person responsible for placing orders?
How does it feel to have full responsibility for order placement?

How often do you order?
What factors affect how frequently you order?

At what times of the year do you order?
Why do you prefer to order in spring instead of fall?

What types of products do you order?
Why do you prefer to order some types of products over others?

Do you meet regularly with your suppliers?
How do feel about regularly scheduled meetings with your suppliers?

Do they offer volume discounts?
What kinds of volume discounts do your current suppliers offer?

Do they deliver in 48 hours or less?
How would you feel about deliveries in 48 hours or less?

Do your orders ever arrive late or damaged?
How do you handle the headaches that come from orders arriving late or damaged?

What percentage of the time?
How do the high percentages of late and damaged goods reflect on your image within the company?

Do your present suppliers assign one individual rep to handle all your needs?
Without assigning individual reps, how have your present suppliers been able to meet your changing needs?

Are you happy with your present suppliers?
What do you like about your present suppliers and what do you dislike?

By now, it should be clear how a combination of closed and open end questions produce a well-rounded exchange of information. To use closed end questions exclusively would be a form of interrogation. To use open end questions before the prospect is willing would appear too personal and certainly be poorly received.

That's why *listening* is the single most important aspect of a prospect call. Inexperienced callers, like many TV reporters and talk show hosts, are often more concerned with what they are going to say next than what the other person has to tell them. Learn to listen for facts, feelings, beliefs, and desires in order to respond and frame your next questions appropriately.

Listen thoroughly and never rush. Thoughtful pauses are an integral part of meaningful conversation. This careful attention to the prospect is critical if you are to discover the ways in which your product or service can best meet his needs.

Positioning Against Your Competition

Finding your prospect has a relationship with one of your competitors is terrific news. Why? Because it is evidence he needs and is willing to pay for your type of product or service—two characteristics of an ideal prospect. Often, such prospects will say they are perfectly satisfied with one of your competitors. To overcome this objection, you must position against the competition in such a way as to demonstrate the advantages of working with you instead.

Never come out and openly challenge the prospect's choice. Instead, use open end questions to probe for the reason behind his selection of your competitor, such as, "If I knew the factors which determine your decisions I could be specific. Can you tell what you like about your present supplier and what you dislike?"

With this information you can move on, without directly challenging his views, to demonstrate the ways customers like him have lost out due to a competitor's lack of what you have. In the following example, Susan B. talks to a floor covering retailer about the industrial rubber flooring he is buying from her competitor:

> "Well, XYZ company certainly is a venerable firm. Many of our current customers used to buy from them, but found they didn't have the luxury of waiting as long as two weeks for delivery. Are you familiar with ABC Floor Covering? They used to buy from XYZ but switched to working with us because they know they can count on competitive pricing and reliable brand name products, and they get them within 48 hours or less. Is quick delivery ever important to you?"

By telling a story or relating a case history you illustrate how a customer might lose out due to the competitor's failure to meet their needs. And you effectively position against the competition without directly challenging your prospect. Just remember, always start out by lightly complimenting your competitors—never by directly criticizing them or the prospect's choice.

The complacent prospect may not switch overnight, but he will know that others—possibly his own competitors— are enjoying the added benefits of working with you. And over time those benefits will be hard to ignore.

Overcoming Objections With "Just Suppose" Questions and Paraphrasing

Through a process of using open and closed end questions and carefully listening to the prospect's responses, you will have gained clear insight to what he might need from you. This is a great time to use a "just suppose" question. These are contingency type questions which insure that the prospect will respond affirmatively—a necessary step if you are to successfully achieve the objective of your cold or warm call.

In the course of her prospect call, Susan has heard, for example, the prospect is saving money on industrial flooring with XYZ company but has repeatedly received late deliveries and is frustrated with XYZ company's limited product lines. She might say, "Just suppose we could offer you special low pricing plus 48-hour delivery on some of the most extensive product lines in the country?" This is bound to get her prospect thinking. How could he respond negatively to something like that? He'll say, "Yeah, I would like that."

If you are listening carefully to the prospect, you should be able to overcome his or her objections with paraphrasing. For example, the national sales manager who says he is too busy to talk to the entrepreneur about the newest territory management software also becomes the perfect candidate for that software if the perceptive entrepreneur says, "There sure is a lot of work here. Are you trying to do it all manually? I'll bet you'd like a way to look at the big picture, manipulate all the detailed data, and still have time left over to manage your guys out in the field, wouldn't you?"

There are many "lead-ins" you can use in paraphrasing. Of course, they all relate back to thinking or feeling, such as, "It sounds as if..." In essence, you've listened beyond the data for emotions and needs. By paraphrasing you will restate and validate those needs and then offer a means to satisfy them. Some of the best "endings" to use in paraphrasing are "...aren't you?" "Isn't that right?" "Really?" or "Isn't that the case?"

For example, Alex S. has cold called the vice president of marketing at a large, multibranch financial institution. While his prospect sounded frazzled and preoccupied at the beginning of the conversation, Alex was able to convince her that what he had to offer was certainly worth a few moments of her time. He has used open and closed end questions to continue qualifying and to discover what his prospect might need from him.

By doing so, Alex has learned a great deal. Throughout, the prospect has presented objections which, from Alex's point of view, demonstrate a strong need for his company's services. The prospect has said she is too busy to meet because her department is understaffed and she has so many different projects for the twenty branch managers. She never knows when the projects will come in and now they have all hit at once. Plus, it's time for her end-of-the-year report to senior management on her department's progress and she is scrambling to recreate all their public relations accomplishments of the past year. Alex responds accordingly:

> "It sounds like you must be incredibly busy working on a half dozen different projects, all unscheduled—especially coming

now at this critical time. And it must be very difficult to have to stop in the middle of all this work and recreate an account- ing of all your PR successes over the past year.... Just suppose you could get management to adopt a branch plan for public relations activities which you could schedule and control? And suppose you had—ready and waiting—PR pros to work alongside your staff during the busiest times. You'd even get monthly summaries to demonstrate your successes year 'round. You'd like that, wouldn't you?"

By effective use of paraphrasing, Alex has demon- strated to the prospect various ways his company can fill her immediate and long-term needs.

On another occasion, Alex is talking with the vice pres- ident of marketing for a residential homebuilder. This pros- pect is responsible for sales in five new home subdivisions and uses an agency for PR as well as advertising and all marketing communications. The prospect says he is happy with the agency's work and his relationship with the agency's president, who gives the account his personal atten- tion. The prospect does admit, however, the last two grand openings the agency handled failed to get the traffic levels they deserved. Alex responds appropriately:

"What I hear you saying is, for the most part you've been happy with your agency relationship and their planning and execution of advertising and direct marketing campaigns. It's unfortunate they haven't been able to produce the same kinds of results for you in the area of special promotions—espe- cially when you have such an excellent product and terrific locations. It sounds like you and your company would ben- efit from the same type of senior level expertise you get from your agency for advertising, but in the areas of special pub- licity and promotions—the kind that will get your new sub- divisions the press and public excitement they deserve.... As you've said, a successful opening can mean the difference between numerous contracts early on and a slow start for the entire project—isn't that right?"

Here, Alex has clearly understood the prospect's satisfaction with his present agency relationship and the quality of their work in all areas but one—special promotions. So Alex doesn't try to "sell" a full-blown, ongoing relationship—something the prospect believes he does not need at this time. Instead, Alex focuses on his own call objective—to get an appointment—and offers a means of satisfying the prospect's needs as he currently perceives them. Later, if Alex has the good fortune to win the special promotion work, he may have the opportunity to expand the relationship and become the builder's full service public relations agency.

Once you have paraphrased your potential customer's responses and overcome every objection using open and closed end questions and "just suppose" statements, you should be ready to close. At this point, if you sense the prospect is still complacent or hesitant, you may ask one further question, such as, "In addition to what we've talked about, is there any other reason why we can't meet your needs?" There really should be no other reason. If there is, address it thoroughly before moving on to your close.

Successful Closing Techniques That Keep You in Control

You've initiated the conversation and guided it through to its moment of truth. Now, focus on your objective and *take action*. When your prospect says, "I can't think of any other reason," it's important to remain in control and ask for exactly what you want.

Ron G.'s warm call objective, you will recall, is to close for an appointment with a well-qualified remodeling prospect. If Ron's warm call has gone well, he should be able to close by simultaneously satisfying the prospect's needs and meeting his own call objective:

"I'll be happy to come by next week and have a closer look at the job. Then we can talk more specifically about how we can build exactly the type of sunroom you're looking for. Is Tuesday at six o'clock good for you?"

If the date and time Ron suggests are unacceptable to his prospect, he will continue naming dates and times until they hit on one that is mutually acceptable. Ron knows never to leave the prospect with the opportunity to say, "Call me next Tuesday and we'll see if that evening is good for me." If Ron were to allow the prospect to take this tack he would find himself in the position of having to repeat the entire process in order to close for an appointment when he called once again on the following Tuesday. Also, as an in-demand professional, Ron's time is valuable and often scheduled far ahead—a fact the prospect should understand and respect. It is always best to suggest penciling in an appointment date and time which may be rescheduled should a conflict arise.

When Ron's warm calling efforts have uncovered a prospect who is well qualified but unprepared to meet due to scheduling or temporary budgetary constraints, he still takes action, laying the groundwork for a future sale by obtaining the best date and time of day for follow-up:

"It sounds as if you've clearly decided to proceed with this type of room addition although the timing may not be right just now. Why don't I call you back around the middle of the month?... Is day or evening best for you?... Great, then I'll talk to you the evening of the fifteenth to set up an appointment for the end of the month."

When cold calling public relations prospects, the objective for Cynthia and Alex is to close for an appointment. But unlike Ron, whose warm call has been a follow-up to a prospect's request, Cynthia and Alex are calling individuals who are generally unfamiliar with their company and have a wide range of PR needs. Alex often finds prospects unwilling to meet with him on his first contact. And he's not surprised. He knows that his first call is just one step in a lengthy selling process.

"It sounds as if a meeting right now would be premature since the grand opening for your next new home subdivision won't be taking place until April. In the meantime, I'll send you a brochure with more important information about my company's services and I'll keep in touch. May I give you a call after the first of the year?... Great, I'll telephone you the week of January fifteenth to talk about the ways we can create a unique grand opening event for Newbury which will generate the right kind of traffic ... and get sales off to a steady start."

For Susan, the objective of a cold call to a prospect who is far flung geographically is to send her product literature along with a quote for purchase of a specific product from a line she represents. As Susan competes predominantly based on price and delivery, her quote, reinforced by the case histories dramatizing the benefits of rapid delivery, should provide the impetus she needs to eventually make a sale. Susan closes her cold call with that in mind:

"It sounds like you'll need twenty entrance mats in the colors we've discussed at least once a month. Why don't I send you a quote on the same mats you've been buying from XYZ company and give you a chance to compare our prices? I'll also send along a catalogue showing the wide range of other products you may want to offer your customers.... We'll send that out overnight this afternoon and then I'll call you at the end of the week to follow up. If you like what you see in our quote and decide to place an order, I can take it from you then over the phone.... There's no rush because, unlike your present supplier, we deliver in just two days from time of order. So instead of trying to decide what you may need two weeks ahead of time, you'll be able to order based on present inventory and get just the number of mats you need.... Is Friday afternoon a good time for me to call you back?"

In each of the preceding three examples, the business owner has told the prospect that he or she will take action either by sending literature, calling back, or keeping an appointment. Following through with the action promised is as important as successful completion of the call itself. Failure to follow through as outlined can undermine your prospect's newly developed confidence in your company and the benefits you have promised.

Since you have initiated and controlled the transaction, the burden of responsibility for its success rests with you. Even when the prospect fails to hold up his or her end of the agreement—such as by failing to be in the office to take your follow-up call or by missing an appointment—it's crucial to remain in control. Refocus and redirect the prospect until your objective has been reached. It may take several—as many as seven or eight—calls before a prospect will include you in the bidding process or place an order, for example. But this type of persistence will pay off.

Twenty Steps to Telephone Success

Before your next cold or warm call, use these twenty points to fine-tune your telephone skills. You'll find they help you better qualify prospects, overcome objections, build long-lasting rapport, and achieve your objectives with surprising ease.

1. Eliminate fear or call reluctance. Never take minor rejection personally. Focus on how much prospects need your expertise. Throw away negative self-images.

2. Project a positive self-image by thinking of prospects as if they were your best friends looking to you for advice.

3. Practice consultative selling. Uncover and fill needs in a friendly, noncombative, and supportive way.

4. Relax and compose a positive affirmation, such as, "I am a competent, confident professional here to help."

5. Compose a mission statement which includes a client or customer benefit. Begin with, "My purpose is to help my clients/customers..."

6. Show enthusiasm for what you do. It's contagious.

7. Be prepared to discuss case histories which reveal the ways you have helped customers or clients meet their goals.

8. Have the ego strength it takes to go on without dwelling on "the one that got away."

9. Cultivate your ego drive. It's what pushes you to look for the next prospect and better ways of meeting his needs.

10. Assess your prospect's needs before picking up the telephone. Ask yourself, "What does he need from me?"

11. Set a realistic call objective which moves your prospect closer to a buying decision.

12. Create an effective opener which includes an introduction of yourself and your company followed by an opening benefit. Write several down and try them out. Then throw away your script.

13. Qualify prospects by asking pertinent questions and listening to the answers.

14. Use closed end questions as conversation starters and to elicit facts.

15. Master the ways open end questions are used to uncover emotional background. Combine open and closed end questions to gain information and build rapport.

16. Listen thoughtfully and never rush.

17. Position against the competition by demonstrating the advantages of working with you instead.

18. Use "just suppose" or other contingency-type questions to ensure prospects will respond affirmatively.

19. Learn to paraphrase using lead-ins and endings to restate and validate prospects' needs and to offer means to satisfy them.

20. Remain in control and take action by closing for your objective.

Breaking Down the Barriers: How To Reach Reluctant Prospects

Sometimes, no matter how you try, you will come across prospects who simply cannot be reached by telephone. Either they refuse to take or return calls from people they don't know, or they are simply inaccessible for long periods of time. In such cases, you may wish to send a letter, wait several days, and then try your call again.

However, *pre-call letters* should never be used as a substitute for cold calls. New home-based business owners, particularly those unfamiliar with sales technique, often use pre-call letters as a type of external crutch to validate their calls. But except when used as a last-ditch effort to reach those prospects who are the most difficult to contact by telephone, pre-call letters can be a costly, time-consuming, and unnecessary step.

Unsolicited letters from unknown companies or individuals are rarely remembered by prospects and are most often discarded by screeners. If you must use a pre-call letter, it's best to make it personal or specifically relevant to the needs of the targeted individual and to follow up within one week.

Now here is an important tip: When following up a pre-call letter, never open with an immediate reference to it. Referring to the letter would make for a weak opener, and a risky one—your prospect may have already forgotten receiving the letter or what it contained. It's best to start out just as you would on a normal cold call. Your strongest opener, of course, always includes your name, an introduction of your company, and an opening benefit. Once the prospect is intrigued with your message and the benefits to be derived from your product or service, you may then reference the letter and its key points.

Screeners can present significant barriers to cold callers, particularly in business-to-businesses sales. Female screeners, including many secretaries and receptionists, are especially hard on women callers. Overall, a secretary's job description may include screening calls for her boss by questioning female and male callers to some degree. But she may be more "zealous" in her efforts when the caller is a woman, perhaps because she feels more comfortable challenging someone she perceives as having lower status or as a peer. Or she may even resent a woman who is a successful executive or business owner.

By and large, women callers are shown less respect than men. This is evidenced by the way they are addressed. For example, secretaries generally refer to male callers by their last names and women callers by their first. When a man calls and announces himself: "This is Wayne Power calling for Jim Hartwell. Is he in this afternoon?" Most often, the secretary will respond, "Just a minute, Mr. Power. I'll see if he's available." The case is different when a woman calls and says, "This is Sandy Power calling for Jim Hartwell. Is he in this afternoon?" The secretary is likely to respond, "Just a minute Sandy and I'll see if he's available. May I say what this is in reference to?"

At times like this it's important to remember, the secretary's attitude is beyond your control. Your own attitude is not. By establishing a positive relationship with the secretary or receptionist, you gain a valuable ally who can actually help you achieve your call objective.

If you are asked, "What is this in regard to?", it is important to convey to the screener in a friendly manner that what you offer is of value. You may respond by saying, "An idea I have that will affect your company's programs." The secretary is not in a position to determine whether your idea is important or not. So generally she will put you through.

If your prospect is unavailable, the secretary may be able to suggest a better day or time for you to call again. In some cases, the secretary may try to redirect your call to a lower authority. For example, Cynthia S., when selling her company's public relations services, most frequently asks for the vice president of marketing. Often, a secretary will respond that the vice president is unavailable and will attempt to put her through to the director of public relations. In situations like this one, Cynthia thanks the secretary and says that she prefers to call back and speak to the vice president when she is available.

You may be tempted to speak with lower level individuals. But beware of getting bogged down with anyone other than the buying authority. Ultimately, you will be limited to that person's weight with his or her own boss when it comes to presenting your product or service. In other words, once you have established a relationship with a lower authority, it may become politically impossible for you to go over his or her head to pitch your business directly to a senior-level decision maker. It is best, therefore, when cold or warm calling to focus on your designated prospect and persevere until you have made satisfactory contact.

Sometimes your prospect, due to time or other constraints, may try to refer you to a lower authority. This often happens to Cynthia when calling PR prospects. She may be talking with a vice president of marketing who attempts to refer her to the director of public relations. When that happens, Cynthia asks the vice president, "If your PR director likes what I have to say, will the door be open for me to come back and present to you?" Cynthia's prospects generally respond favorably to this type of question. And so will yours.

Should you find yourself in this situation, ask the senior executive if she will alert her subordinate to your upcoming call. With this implied endorsement from the senior executive—the buying authority—you'll be well on your way to winning the new business essential to growing your company.

chapter four

Ten Steps to Successful Meetings

Chances are you've spent countless hours planning, taking, or giving meetings your entire working life. Yet, unless you are already a professional salesperson, you will quickly find that business ownership mandates a new set of meeting techniques which energize and motivate prospects. Once learned, you'll find these new skills complement those you have traditionally used to guide or persuade supervisors, colleagues, and staff.

You may be wondering, after all these years of meeting experience, why learn new techniques now? In fact, there are two dramatically compelling reasons:

- the level of sophisticated competition
- the high cost of selling

No matter whether you're selling to other businesses or to consumers at home, you will meet with substantial competition in every business arena. Many of your competitors will be highly trained in sales technique, and busy prospects will have little patience with any business owner or representative who poorly manages the initial sales transaction.

The second and even more compelling reason to become skilled in meeting techniques is cost. The average cost of a sales call—leaving one's office to meet with a prospect—

is at an all-time high. National figures show that for most industries it runs into hundreds of dollars. And for home-based business owners, the cost of a sales call—particularly an unsuccessful one—is virtually incalculable when it has taken the place of other income-generating activities. Since prospect meetings are not only essential to the growth of your company but to its very survival, you must make the most of each meeting in order to maximize your return on every dollar invested in travel, materials and, most of all, time.

What follows are ten important guidelines for successful new business meetings. In a way, they are a bit like the original Ten Commandments. When a first meeting with a prospect goes terribly awry and the walls come tumbling down, it can often be directly traced back to breaking one of these ten rules. Outside of new business, you'll find these techniques come in handy in a lot of "ordinary" meetings as well. Best of all, once adopted, these guidelines are very easy to live with.

1. Meet only with qualified prospects.
2. Set a goal for every meeting.
3. Plan the meeting in advance.
4. Come prepared with tools, materials, and "personal polish."
5. Use property observations.
6. Guide the exchange with open and closed end questions.
7. Listen carefully and treat objections as opportunities.
8. Be intuitive—probe for spoken and unspoken objections.
9. Close by proposing solutions.
10. Take positive action.

Meet Only With Qualified Prospects

Before ever leaving your office to meet face-to-face with any prospect, you will have completed a qualifying cold or warm call. You'll have learned as much about the prospect as possible, determined what her potential needs might be and whether she has the ability to pay for your product or service. It's not critical that the prospect be "ready to buy," only that she have the ability and some predisposition to do so prior to your first meeting.

Be certain to draw a clear distinction between prospect qualifications and objections. For example, a prospect who says she is happy using the services of your competition, but is still willing to meet, is indeed well qualified. She has a need and is capable of paying for your services. However, her expressed satisfaction with your competitor is an objection—one which you may successfully overcome in your first meeting.

On the other hand, a prospect who has never purchased a product or service similar to yours and is uncertain how an appropriate budget will be allocated is not well qualified, despite his lack of objections or his willingness to meet with you. This prospect may well be a time waster.

Often, the most successful home-based business owners are also those who expend great effort to qualify prospects carefully. They know that good prospects are most likely to turn into great clients.

Daryl R. owns and operates a computer maintenance business staffed with as many as five independent technicians who are also based in their own homes. While Daryl's ultimate customer is the personal computer owner, his prospects are the computer resellers—retailers who may sell one PC or fifty to business customers. When the retailer sells the hardware, Daryl's company supplies the PC maintenance contract, placing him and his technicians on call for a monthly fee.

Daryl takes extensive care to identify and target his primary reseller prospects. He has acquired a list of the top computer resellers in his market area and eliminated all those who do not fit his volume qualification and other criteria. He cold calls the presidents and key decision makers at his target companies. This qualifying cold call is followed by direct mailings at regular intervals and, ultimately, a follow-up call, which often yields an appointment. So Daryl's prospects have been qualified an average of three times prior to any face-to-face meetings.

Linda K., the newsletter publisher introduced in Chapter 1, targets only those public interest groups and large associations which are already publishing national newsletters. Linda's expertise lies in taking over, upgrading, and streamlining both the publications and, consequently, their readership. As Linda formulates her prospect list, she acquires samples of these organizations' newsletters, and speaks directly to the ways she can help improve them during her initial cold calls. While qualifying prospects, Linda gently hints at the ways she might help improve their organizations' newsletters without ever directly criticizing them. This strategy generally yields appointments with highly qualified, interested prospects.

Set a Goal for Every Meeting

The first step in planning an effective prospect meeting is to set an achievable, realistic goal. First meeting goals will vary greatly by company depending upon the industry and type of business. But in some way the goal must encompass moving the prospect incrementally closer to a purchase. For some, the first face-to-face meeting with a prospect offers the opportunity to qualify further, establish a relationship, and prepare for a major presentation. For others, their product or service is such that they must close the sale at the very first meeting.

Make a list of what you plan to accomplish in the first face-to-face meeting with your prospective clients or customers. Focus on your principal objectives, and tailor your entire approach accordingly.

Hunter C. is a landscape architect who, with his partner, Rosemary, and an office manager, works from a dramatic sky-lit carriage house adjacent to his home. The carriage house office is surrounded by extensively landscaped grounds, including three garden rooms with gazebo, contemporary sculpture and a reflecting pond.

For Hunter's landscape architectural firm, leads are generated by marketing communications—public relations exposure from a major landscape architectural award and an interview in the Home section of the metropolitan area daily newspaper. Leads must be carefully qualified by the office manager, as Hunter's clients will pay $5,000 for initial planning and design plus the cost of creating the garden landscape.

Only those who fit the narrow prospect profile are referred to Hunter or Rosemary for warm calls, and the remainder are politely referred elsewhere. The warm call objective is to continue qualifying and close for an initial meeting at the prospective client's site.

During the first meeting with the prospective client, Hunter will work toward positioning his company as the client's best choice. He'll probe for the client's tastes, budget, time frame, the desired level of maintenance, the client's vision of the finished garden, and whether the job may include adding hardscapes such as walls and permanent walkways or elements such as a pool or tennis court. Ultimately, though, Hunter's goal is always the same: to close by reviewing the $5,000 initial architectural planning and design fee and arrange for a second meeting. This second meeting will begin with a tour of his own expansive garden and culminate with a contract agreement signed in his carriage house.

Newsletter publisher Linda K. will also require more than one face-to-face meeting with a prospect in order to obtain a contract. For Linda, the goal of the first meeting is to develop a relationship, continue qualifying, and lay the groundwork for a future presentation in which she will demonstrate her ideas and capabilities. In the first meeting, Linda must probe for client desires, budgets, names of decision makers and influencers, the client's past experiences with the newsletter, circulation goals, the competition Linda may face in securing the contract, the prospective client's time frame and many other factors. She will close by setting a date for a major presentation at which she will present a complete composite, sample editorial content, paper samples, PMS (color) recommendations, and a budget proposal, in addition to case histories and past work samples.

Unlike Hunter and Linda, Daryl's goal is to close the sale on his very first sales call. If you recall, he has extensively qualified his prospects and used marketing communications and follow-up calls. In his first face-to-face meetings with his prospects, he offers a thirty-day free trial for up to ten PCs on one computer maintenance contract. His prospects have everything to gain and little to lose. Consequently, Daryl often achieves his goal.

Plan the Meeting in Advance

Everyone has met, in his or her business life, a Wesley Wingit. These are the individuals who never plan ahead and prefer to fly by the seats of their pants, mistaking disorganization and lack of focus for adventure and excitement.

In the corporate world, Wesley Wingits may at times do well, thanks to the supporting structure of well-organized secretaries, assistants, and other subordinates. As home-based business owners, Wesley Wingits get into deep trouble. Despite their usual charisma or charm, prospects respond poorly to their careless, off-the-cuff approach.

To be successful, a prospect meeting always requires some level of planning. It's best to begin by reviewing the prospect information, including call reports, to determine what the prospect's needs are most likely to be. Then think specifically about what you can do to help your prospect achieve her goals. Review case histories and think about the ways you have solved similar challenges for other customers or clients. Linda, for example, reviews four or five of the newsletters her company publishes for existing clients and selects two examples, mentally reviewing these case histories to touch on salient points of special interest to her prospect.

When planning your prospect meeting, formulate a mental checklist of the steps you must take in order to achieve your own objective. If these steps include qualifying the prospect according to a lengthy series of criteria, you may wish to jot them down to use as a guide during the meeting.

Structure the meeting so that it fits within the prospect's schedule. If your meeting is too brief or hurried, it may indicate to the prospect a lack of depth or planning. On the other hand, if your meeting is structured to go on for a long period, it may be best to determine in advance the amount of time the prospect has to spend with you. Then you will be able to carefully manage the time you spend in his office. Dragging out a meeting shows a lack of respect for the prospective client's time. And may provoke anger or resentment.

Daryl's meetings with computer retailers often take place in busy offices behind retail showrooms, or sometimes out on the selling floor. So he has learned to structure a brief presentation which contains an overview of all the facts and brings him to a close within a manageable period of time. If the prospect would like to continue, then Daryl is free to elaborate and expand his presentation accordingly. Hunter, on the other hand, must plan to spend large chunks of time with his affluent prospective customers. They expect focused, personalized attention and lengthy discussions relating to aesthetics.

Come Prepared With Tools, Materials, and "Personal Polish"

Owners of home-based businesses must rely on tools which communicate solidarity and permanence, plus any other attributes of their particular field. Tools validate the impression of your company as a viable, growing concern. Your brochure, price list, portfolio, presentation folders, and other materials all create a visual identity which must stand in place of high-profile executive offices or a large retail storefront. Your tools have to stand up against those of your most successful out-of-home–based competitor in the areas of quality and professionalism.

For example, computer retailers might be less willing to accept Daryl's thirty-day free trial if his price list were just a typed and copied page instead of his well-designed sheet printed in two colors on glossy stock. Daryl's polished materials reinforce the high-quality image he has created for his company. An investment in quality sales tools is like an investment in good clothes. They both make the right impression and wear well over time.

Personal polish is a combination of appearance and attitude. For many, one of the greatest perks of working from home is the lack of a formal dress code. At home, shorts, sweats, blue jeans, sweaters, whatever type of clothing is most comfortable and supports your positive frame of mind may be worn as you like—provided clients or customers will not be meeting with you in your home.

But when meeting with prospects, appearance does count. Be aware of the total impression you create. Prospects buy the impression of you as the image of your company overall, and it must be a competent and professional one. As a business owner, you may choose to discard the old corporate dress code and let your personal creativity and taste shine through. But individuality does not necessarily mean informality, and your appearance, whatever your line of work, should be appropriate to the situation. Daryl feels it is most appropriate to meet with his retail prospects in a traditional suit and tie, while Hunter visits prospective clients dressed in a sport coat with an open collar. Each is dressed differently yet appropriately for the situation, and each has personal polish.

In addition to your personal appearance, anything you carry with you to a prospect meeting should reflect your personal polish. If you carry a briefcase, make sure it is neat. When you open it, do hundreds of small papers fall out? Is the appointment book in which you jot down the prospect's next meeting well organized? Personal polish can go a long way toward overcoming any negative images your prospect may hold of home-based businesses and the professionalism of their owners.

The same basic attitudinal rules hold for home-based business owners as for any others: Be on time, be honest, don't over-promise, don't use profane language, and never show disrespect. If you are new to visiting prospects, you'll want to learn to treat everyone in the prospect's organization as if he or she were the buying authority. You are selling an image of yourself and your company from the moment you walk in the door. While you are an expert in your own field, this does not denigrate those who are less expert.

When visiting a prospective client or customer in a business setting, friendliness to everyone, including the person at the front desk and those you meet in the hallways, will pay off. The receptionist may be the president's daughter. The head of sales, his brother-in-law. Anyone in the company may exert his or her influence to help or hinder you.

The same holds true when visiting consumers in their homes. If the husband is your principal prospect and you denigrate the wife, it's unlikely she will want you in her home. And her husband will surely hear about it.

When preparing for your prospect meeting, organize all your sales tools and materials (samples, presentation boards, charts, portfolios, etc.) back in your own office well in advance. Then do a mental check, running through your list to devise a tentative order for your presentation. This structure or organization should, of course, remain flexible, as you will adjust and tailor your meeting or presentation to the responses and needs of your prospect.

Just about the only thing that will rarely change is the timing for presentation of your business card. If you are like most business people, you'll find the best time to present your business card is when you enter and introduce yourself. This will help the prospect to remember your name. Plus, a well-produced card will begin to reinforce the image of your company as polished and professional right from the start. It's particularly important to present your business card as a means of identification when selling to consumers, such as when a male business owner calls on a woman in her home. In this instance, it's a good idea to present the card prior to entry.

Prepare for your prospect meeting by deciding not only what materials you will present and when, but also how you will present them. Presentation materials are like musical instruments. You will essentially be judged by how well you play. If you are using charts, photographs, a portfolio, or presentation boards, rehearsal is important. To avoid a disorganized presentation or unwieldy use of materials, walk through your presentation step by step. Practice holding and displaying the materials and practice your narration, editing out extraneous actions or descriptions.

Make certain your materials are "presentation ready." That means they must be tailored to your prospect, professional-looking, clean, and ready for close scrutiny.

Linda utilizes samples of newsletters she has revised and reissued, and presents case histories which are particularly relevant to each individual prospect. She has prepared professional-looking presentation boards with before-and-after examples. Each board contains the original newsletter on the left and her upgraded version on the right. Both are mounted inside transparent sleeves so they may be easily removed and reviewed by prospects. Next to each are corresponding stats showing before-and-after figures for increased circulation and decreased cost per piece. Overall, the "presentation ready" boards and Linda's approach to using successful case histories make an impressive presentation.

Use Property Observations

Once on your prospect's turf, you will be able to observe items in the surroundings which provide clues to her as an individual. When visiting a prospective client's office, the surroundings will tell you just about everything you need to know about her power within the organization and the priority she places on various aspects of her lifestyle. Make mental note of awards on the walls as well as pictures of family members or sports trophies.

Certainly you will never force personal information out of a prospect or your own information on her. But at some point in the conversation you should find the opportunity to tell an anecdote which relates something of you as a likable person that makes a connection. This should tie in with what you believe is important to the prospect. For example, when meeting with a prospective client in her quiet, spacious home, Hunter might immediately pick up on the classical music playing on the stereo. He might then make a polite inquiry and perhaps make reference to something in his own background which would put him on a more personal or familiar basis with his prospect, such as his own personal enjoyment of Vivaldi.

Property observations will stand you in good stead in the long run. If you have noticed an autographed baseball in your prospect's office, for example, further discussion may uncover your mutual enjoyment of the sport. This can provide the common ground for a friendlier relationship. Then when calling to follow up on your initial meeting, a reference to the prospect's favorite team's most recent win will reestablish that connection—and will help you form a more lasting relationship with a prospect who may indeed become a client.

Property observations are integral to Daryl's success in first meetings with prospects. By noting the busy or sometimes frantic nature of the retailer's showroom and back office, he can easily relate specific examples of how his computer maintenance service will provide relief.

Guide the Exchange With Open and Closed End Questions

Confronted with such an obvious need for his services, Daryl might ask,

> "Is Fred here your sole PC maintenance person?... How many calls does he get for assistance on an average day?... How do your customers feel about having to wait two or three days before Fred has the time to address their problems?... It sounds like maintenance support would really help cut down on angry customers and eliminate your need to add a second PC maintenance person, wouldn't it?"

By using a series of closed and open end questions, Daryl has addressed his prospect's immediate need and provided a means for filling it in a way that is advantageous both in terms of satisfying customers and cutting costs.

Even businesspeople who are uncomfortable using open end questions on the telephone feel more at ease using them in one-on-one meetings with prospects. Face-to-face with an individual, you are less likely to feel pressured to follow a script or to perform and more likely to relax and let your natural conversational style come through. Most successful businesspeople have the ability to build rapport on a variety of levels. Often, the components are a mixture of self-respect, responsiveness, consideration for others, and a generally pleasant personality coupled with a sense of humor.

Hunter's clients appreciate his relaxed, easy-going style, and much of his success can be attributed to his ability to use open end questions which reveal emotions and deep-seated preferences. It's not surprising his clients find the garden environments Hunter designs for them to be satisfying to their souls as well as their senses.

Listen Carefully and Treat Objections as Opportunities

For Hunter, the client who objects to an intricate garden design because she is concerned about the high maintenance of such an environment provides an excellent opportunity for him to design with low-maintenance native plants which are more drought resistant—and more exciting to him conceptually than just another English-style cottage garden. Like Hunter, your prospects' objections may provide opportunities for you to solve their problems in more creative ways.

One professional association prospect with whom Linda was meeting objected strongly to revamping or expanding her organization's newsletter, until Linda suggested creating an electronic newsletter which would be sent on-line and downloaded by modem at member organizations. As the association's membership consisted of individuals and companies whose livelihood is based on use of such technology, this would save Linda's prospect huge sums in postage and printing while actually enabling the organization to expand its newsletter's readership.

There are no insuperable objections, problems, or challenges—just opportunities for good listeners and aggressive entrepreneurs.

Be Intuitive—Probe for Spoken and Unspoken Objections

Once inside your prospect's office or home, you have many positive advantages which you didn't have when talking with him on the telephone. First, you claim his full attention and you may observe body language, noting how the prospect responds to your presentation. A good listener is highly empathic and senses the reactions of others. Empathy is a guidance mechanism which allows you to follow through each of the prospect's objections until the real underlying needs are targeted.

Focus on the signals your prospect is sending you with his body, with his head. Is he sitting through your presentation shaking his head from left to right without expressing a definite objection? It's best to respond to unspoken objections by using closed and open end questions to draw out your prospect and find out what his underlying concerns may be.

Daryl has been meeting with a prospect for over thirty minutes. During most of that period, the prospect has been jumping out of his chair and pacing nervously, from time to time glancing over his shoulder at several other individuals sitting in the tiny office space behind the busy showroom. Yet the prospect is not verbally objecting to anything in Daryl's presentation. In fact, Daryl has had great difficulty in eliciting much response whatsoever.

Knowing that a lack of objections can also mean the prospect has clearly made up his mind not to use his services, Daryl feels it's best to uncover the prospect's underlying objection in order that he may address and overcome it:

"While you seem to appreciate the value of my company's services, something is clearly concerning you. May I ask—does what I'm presenting make sense to you from an economic standpoint?... And yet you still have additional questions in your mind, isn't that right? What concerns you?"

As it turns out, his prospect's brother-in-law directly handles PC maintenance and his sister is sitting in the office behind them listening to Daryl's presentation. Now the prospect's nervous behavior makes perfect sense. Daryl suggests the following:

"Just suppose we could structure a maintenance support agreement which would enhance your brother-in-law's ability to head a successful, growing division of your company. That type of arrangement would satisfy everyone concerned, wouldn't it?"

Cultivate your own intuitive qualities and learn to be an empathic person, using all of your energy to focus on your prospect. Empathic people sit forward in their chairs and make eye contact with their prospects. They listen.

Close by Proposing Solutions

If you have followed the preceding eight guidelines for successful first meetings, including using open and closed end questions and converting objections to opportunities, your prospect will now see your product or service as indispensable. Indeed, without it, his needs will not be met.

When your product or service is well matched to fit the prospect's needs, the "solution" is satisfaction of those needs—and it can only be derived by working with you and your company.

- Daryl's solution is to provide a 30-day free trial for up to ten PCs.

- Linda's solution is to offer a complete presentation which demonstrates the ways in which the prospect organization can dramatically increase the performance of its newsletter.

- Hunter closes with the promise of creating a garden to reflect the deepest aspirations and character of its owner. For the prospect, the next step to reaching this solution is to visit Hunter's own garden to view individual plants and garden themes. There, they will quickly formalize a contract to initiate their work together.

In other words, the solution you close with should both fill your meeting objective and satisfy the prospect's needs. But no matter how well qualified, not every prospect will be right for you, nor you and your company for every prospect. During the course of your meeting, you may meet with resistance too strong to overcome, preventing achievement of your first meeting goal. If you have been listening carefully, you should still be able to propose a solution which in some way continues to move the prospect closer to a buying decision.

When Hunter finds a prospect to be fully qualified yet resistant to his suggestions or his personal or horticultural design style, he closes by proposing a follow-up meeting between the prospect and his partner, Rosemary. Hunter hopes Rosemary's design style, plant material preferences or personality may be more to the prospect's liking.

When Linda's prospect objects to scheduling a complete presentation due, for example, to temporary budget constraints, Linda remains focused on her ultimate goal. She has determined that the prospect's funding difficulties are temporary and within three months the prospect will be able to take a complete presentation. So, Linda's solution is to propose a series of activities including using the 90-day period to become expert on the prospect's competition and challenges; scheduling an interim meeting to discuss editorial issues and preliminary concepts; mailing him samples of other clients' newsletters from which he may draw ideas; and, finally, scheduling the complete presentation for 90 to 120 days in the future.

In both instances, the prospects have clearly defined needs. It's up to Hunter and Linda to close by providing solutions their prospects will accept.

Take Positive Action

As in any successful relationship, your actions will speak louder than the promises you've made in your initial prospect meeting. Follow-through with the promised action is critical.

If, for example, Linda promises to return within two weeks with a full-blown presentation, but calls a week later and schedules the presentation for three to four weeks in the future, she will undermine the prospect's belief in her ability to follow through. Or, should she come in on time with a presentation but fail to include the information agreed upon in the prospect meeting, Linda will once again lessen her chances for success. No matter how creative her samples or impressive the materials, failure to follow through with the promises made in the initial meeting could cost her the relationship.

Once Daryl has successfully closed with his prospect—and the prospect has agreed to award him a PC maintenance contract for one of his customers—he takes immediate action. Upon signature of the contract, Daryl asks to meet with others in the new client's company with whom he might work and supplies them with Rolodex cards and rate sheets exactly as promised. These meetings may take place immediately, or Daryl may return in a day or two. This provides him another opportunity to discuss even more recent sales, and offer to expedite additional or multiple contracts.

In the weeks that follow, Daryl and his technicians have the opportunity to prove their expertise and establish a pleasant working relationship with all points of contact at the retail operation. Now, Daryl simply supplies the sales and/or bookkeeping departments there with the paperwork they need in order to initiate contracts for new customers.

From his first meeting, Daryl demonstrated his ability to take action and follow through on promises. And, as a result of his careful follow-through plus the good work he and his technicians have provided, Daryl has acquired an ongoing, lucrative relationship with his new client.

Even after an unsuccessful first meeting with the prospect—one in which the prospect does not allow you to achieve your objective—taking action is still important. A prospect's needs may change rapidly in response to the market, competition, turnover, and a wide range of other factors. If you have created a positive impression in your meeting, then the action you take next will reinforce that positive image. And when the prospect is in a position to find the benefits of your product or service more compelling, he or she may become a customer or client.

When you have closed by providing a solution other than one which meets your primary objective, describe for the prospect exactly what course of action you plan to take. Then follow through in a timely manner. Hunter, for example, moves quickly to set up a meeting between the prospect and his partner, Rosemary, in hopes of salvaging the relationship before the prospect selects another landscape architectural firm.

The follow-up action you suggest will vary depending upon the level of interest exhibited by your prospect. For those the farthest from making a buying decision, taking action can be as simple as promising to add them to your list to receive regular mailings or agreeing upon the best month for telephone follow-up.

Think back to your last unsuccessful prospect meeting. Would adherence to these ten guidelines have improved the results? If your last prospect meeting went well, consider whether, with incorporation of these techniques, it might have gone even better. And start practicing these new business meeting survival skills now to produce the results you need from your next prospect meeting.

chapter five

Making Presentations That Sell

Warren D. stands just to the right of his large easel, which for the moment displays nothing but a pad of big blank sheets. Around the table in this small, utilitarian conference room sit the seven owners and managers of his industrial machinery manufacturing prospect. Among them is the company's founder and chairman, now in his seventies, his son and daughter who jointly run the 37-year-old, $42 million company, a first cousin who manages plant operations, and three others who head key departments. The relationships among all of the individuals in this group are highly complex, with occasional jockeying for position among the family members, and non-family members struggling to overcome barriers—both perceived and real—of their own.

As a management consultant, it's Warren's job to use this presentation to demonstrate the ways he can help their company increase production and profitability while functioning effectively within the complexity and limitations of the group. For this purpose, Warren has chosen to use a style of presentation with which he is uniquely comfortable. Using blank sheets—or flip charts—suspended from an easel, Warren outlines, or "demonstrates," his strategy step-by-step, inviting comment and input throughout the presentation.

This highly interactive process involves everyone in the room. Their thoughts are noted on the rapidly filling pages and become as integral to the quickly evolving "presentation" as his own. Within 45 minutes or so, Warren has learned as much about his prospective clients as they have about his strategies for increasing their business success. And the synergy which has developed has laid a solid foundation for their future working relationship. At the close, Warren simply sets a date to proceed with their work together, regarding further comment and feedback as a prelude to their first official working session.

The Key to Successful Sales Presentations and Seminars

Like Warren, home-based business owners most often make presentations to directly sell their products and services—or to obtain funding. Other types of group presentations, such as seminars and speaking engagements, allow business owners to indirectly sell their products or services by positioning themselves as expert sources of information. Sales presentations and seminars are both excellent opportunities to sell and must become a part of your overall sales strategies. Goals and tactics, however, differ widely:

- The goals of a sales presentation are to persuade, then motivate, and finally, enlighten.
- The goals of a seminar are first to enlighten, motivate, and then persuade.

To be successful, a sales presentation must persuade the audience that what you have or want is of value. They must be so motivated to accept your "solution" that they believe their needs will not be met without it. Finally, an effective sales presentation always enlightens the audience, helping them to see the resolution of a challenge in a new or unique way.

Conversely, the first duty of a seminar is to enlighten. After all, a seminar is by its nature an opportunity to be informed or educated. The seminar audience must be motivated to use their new-found knowledge or information. Ultimately, they will be persuaded that the seminar host is an expert, an authority to be sought out when further information or expertise in this area is desired.

Clearly, seminar and sales presentation tactics are not interchangeable. For example, a seminar may, due to its method of presentation, be entertaining and enjoyable. But while a presentation may in some cases be enjoyable, an "entertaining" business presentation is usually one which fails so badly in its attempt to persuade, it amuses the participants.

Six Ingredients of a Winning Sales Presentation

Here are six comments you should look forward to hearing from your audience following your next sales presentation:

1. **"The presentation demonstrated an understanding of our industry and type of business."** The presentation must reflect an understanding of the challenges faced by your prospects as they relate to their industry, competition, marketplace, and other factors. If you are an expert, be sure to structure your presentation to allow your knowledge and experience to shine through. If you are inexperienced with your prospects' industry or type of business but expert at supplying the product or service they need, structure the presentation to focus on your strengths. But do your homework and gain as much information and background as possible without hands-on experience.

2. **"The presentation directly addressed our needs."** Your presentation must speak directly to the benefits your prospects will derive by using your product or

service. Prior to your presentation, you spent considerable time on the telephone and in face-to-face meetings with your prospects and, by now, have a clear picture of what their organization might need from you. Your presentation must communicate step-by-step the actions you will take to satisfy those needs.

3. "Staffing and support were adequately addressed." Home-based businesses often operate with small or limited staffs. Consequently, home-based business owners may tend to omit the subject of staffing and support from their sales presentations in fear of "scaring off" the prospects. And prospects may be justifiably concerned about adequate staffing but fail to raise the objection for fear of embarrassing the presenter. As unspoken objections linger and grow, it is always best to address how you plan to staff and support the prospects' work once they become clients.

4. "The presentation provided reasonable solutions." The solutions you propose for satisfying the prospects' needs must appear logical, acceptable, and, above all, reasonable. To offer solutions which are unrealistic or untenable by virtue of cost or other factors will invalidate an otherwise solid presentation.

5. "He/she took time to get to know us." Since prospects hire people, not companies, and since they hire people they like, it's fundamentally important to allow time before, during, and after your presentation to relate to them as individuals. This is extremely difficult when the audience is quite large. But under normal circumstances, such as in a room with as few as two, or as many as ten people, the prospects should feel they have come to know something of you personally. And you must demonstrate an interest in getting to know them on that individual level as well.

Prior to your presentation, take pains to shake hands with and greet each person present. Depending upon the format of your presentation, you may wish to draw out individuals at key points or encourage questions through-out. And always leave enough time after your pitch to take questions, *ask* questions, and converse informally. The success of this exchange can make or break your presentation, and its importance must never be overlooked.

6. "The leave-behind summarized the presentation well and provided helpful background data." Your leave-behind must stand alone as your representative during the days and sometimes weeks following your major presentation. Individuals who were unable to attend your sales presentation will rely on it for information, and those who were in attendance will review your leave-behind to refresh their memories. This is particularly valid when you are in a competitive situation and your audience may—after taking three or four presentations—begin to confuse some of your key points.

Your leave-behind must not only look good, but it must also sell for you. It should carefully summarize your presentation plus provide background which will help support your company as the prospects' best choice. To save time and effort in the long run, create a "standard" leave-behind format and company boilerplate which may include company and personal background data, references, case histories, and so forth. Then, customize your leave-behind for each presentation, adapting the body to summarize each new proposal. Your leave-behind should be creatively consistent in appearance with the group of tools you have developed to build your company image, as well as comprehensive and error free.

Six Characteristics of a Successful Seminar

Under the best circumstances, getting thorough feedback on a seminar you've delivered can be most difficult. Unlike a sales presentation where an "excellent pitch" produces rather immediate results, feedback from even a top-notch seminar can be long in coming and spotty at best. So to give you an idea of what an audience is really looking for, here are the comments you might overhear following an excellent seminar:

1.   "The information was comprehensive and instructive." For a seminar to enlighten, it must cover the topic thoroughly, be well researched, and instruct the audience on a level consistent with their knowledge and expertise. Before developing any seminar, it's important to evaluate the proficiency level of the prospective audience. Then prepare to comprehensively address the topic by supplying information specific to your audience's needs and capabilities. Try not to present information which is either too basic or too technical—both are boring and rarely instructive.

2.   "The information was well supported by specifics or examples." To be clearly understood, general information should be supported by relevant examples. The difference between a good seminar and a bad seminar is often determined by the way the presenter breaks up the facts by presenting stories, case histories, or anecdotes which help the audience relate to the factual information. In many cases, examples drawn from your own past experience will help position you as knowledgeable and expert. And by presenting stories or case histories which reflect the achievements of yourself or others, you may motivate audience members to act on the information you impart.

3.   "The presentation had a logical flow and was easy to follow." Structure and organize your presentation so that your information seems to flow naturally. Good presentations are never choppy and don't hop back and forth from one point to another. The information seems to flow step by step in a logical, easy-to-follow manner. When preparing your presentation, think about your topic as if you were learning about it for the very first time. Look for clear, overriding principles or guidelines which can provide the structure of your presentation. Summarize your key points or guidelines at the outset of your presentation. Flesh them out logically step-by-step and then summarize the key points in your conclusion. This will help even the neophyte follow and understand your seminar.

4. **"The presentation style was interesting/never boring."** The words *informational* and *educational* should never be synonymous with the words *dull* or *boring*. Create a visual presentation which compels your audience to follow your seminar intently. The visual presentation itself is merely the combination of the presenter's "performance" or skill in front of the audience and her effective use of tools and materials, such as slides or videotapes. Physical and verbal mannerisms such as hiding tensely behind a large podium or reading in a monotone fashion from a typed script will cause your audience to "tune out" and ignore what might otherwise be excellent information.

Select presentation tools appropriate to the setting, the subject, and your personal presentation style. If your seminar is technical, avoid visuals which focus heavily on figures or dense copy. Focus instead on visuals which represent broader concepts or summarize facts.

When using visual aids such as slides or transparencies for a seminar presentation of twenty minutes or more, it's best to cluster the visuals during segments of your presentation. Turning down the lights for more than twenty minutes can put an audience to sleep, and losing eye contact with you for that period may cause their interest to wane. By clustering your visuals during segments of your presentation, you also effectively reduce the number of slides and transparencies required to create a compelling presentation. And it's important to remember never to leave a static visual on screen for a lengthy period of time. In an age when television commercials tell an entire story in thirty seconds, just one minute spent looking at the same static visual image can leave an audience groaning and restless.

For major seminars or speaking engagements, such as at a regional or national trade show, consider mixing media. For example, the presentation might open with a short, exciting videotape viewed on strategically placed monitors. Follow this by entering through the audience using a cordless microphone and introducing yourself from a stage without a podium. Begin your oral presentation without visuals and then step down into the audience and to the side to continue while slides are projected on the screen at the rear of the stage. Following the slide segment, use a second video clip to close the formal presentation. Then remount the stage to take questions and directly address the audience's needs. While such an elaborate presentation may be outside of your present budget, consider carefully how you will combine your personal presentation style with visual tools and materials to create seminars which are both educational and interesting.

5. "The presenter was expert and knowledgeable." An effective seminar demonstrates the knowledge and expertise of the presenter. By thoroughly covering the topic, thoughtfully and comprehensively addressing audience questions, and by presenting appropriate case histories or anecdotes, you will convince the audience that what you know or have to say is of significant value. Unlike a sales presentation, a seminar is an inappropriate place for lengthy presentation of personal credentials or achievements. That would be viewed in this context as boastful or pushy. Instead, a thorough demonstration of your knowledge will essentially position you as expert.

A brief leave-behind—whether prepared by you or the seminar organizers—should include a summary of your company's capabilities or your bio and personal credentials along with a prominently displayed telephone number. Again, this must be written subtly and avoid any appearance of a "sales pitch."

6. **"The question-and-answer period directly addressed my needs."** A question-and-answer period allows the audience a critical opportunity to make the information they have obtained relevant to their own personal situations. This short period also allows you the opportunity to make personal, one-on-one contact with members of the audience and to demonstrate the wide range of your knowledge and your ability to formulate solutions. It will help to anticipate the types of questions audience members might ask when you prepare for the seminar and to do any additional research accordingly.

Both sales presentations and seminars or speaking engagements are excellent opportunities to sell your company's product or service. By understanding the tactical differences between them, you can successfully tailor any type of presentation to effectively win over your audience and elicit positive responses.

Think back to your last group presentation. What was the audience or prospect organization's reaction? In your last seminar, did the audience feel they were getting a sales pitch? When you last made a sales presentation to a group of prospects, was there an enthusiastic exchange or did they sit back coolly, as if responding to a speech or lecture? If your most recent group presentations met with these types of negative responses, now is an excellent time to rethink your tactics and develop presentations that will better meet the needs of your audiences—and increase your company's sales.

Three Factors That Make or Break Group Presentations

The three principal components of any successful presentation are:

- content
- structure
- style

Here are two examples of the ways these factors are interwoven to create winning presentations.

Terri L. is a retail sales consultant who has, over the past five years, built a strong reputation and a successful home-based practice by helping her department store clients improve customer service nationwide. Right now she is making a sales presentation to eleven senior executives of a venerable department store chain. In recent years, their stores have been experiencing a significant decline in sales, in part because of nationwide expansion of a competing chain renowned for its superior customer service and satisfaction. Among the eleven executives present, several have been charged with the task of evaluating the cost to upgrade customer service throughout all stores and to reposition the chain—versus an immediate sale of the entire chain to a conglomerate. The latter is a choice no one in the room would like to make, and all are focused intently on what Terri has to tell them.

During her one-hour presentation, Terri demonstrates her understanding of the challenges faced by her prospect, enumerates them one by one, and through use of case histories and relevant examples shows how she has solved similar challenges for other department store chains. She shows the benefits clients have derived by using her consultative services, presenting increased sales figures to illustrate the positive results of her team's efforts. And, finally, she closes by proposing a program of activities to upgrade the chain's customer service nationwide. Her solutions are accompanied by related costs and time frames for execution of the work.

This, of course, describes the *content* of her presentation. This data or solid information is presented in a *style* which is involving and compelling. Terri's tools consist of a combination of presentation boards and videotape.

The videotape, which is run on two monitors to accommodate the eleven-person audience, demonstrates Terri's methods of working with department store staff and managers. Clips include footage of customer focus groups conducted to gauge store customers' impressions of service and personnel, examples of role playing techniques shot behind the scenes during training sessions, and footage of newly retrained employees smoothly interacting with customers. The six-minute videotape is presented in two three-minute parts at appropriate points during Terri's presentation. Use of videotape footage gives her prospects an opportunity to "experience" what working with Terri and her team might be like and to witness firsthand the benefits to be derived by undertaking a program like the one she proposes.

Terri breaks up her tape, even though it is only six minutes, in order to keep her audience focused on her and to continue the momentum she has built up in her oral presentation. An easel and boards are used throughout to outline her proposed solutions and present large color graphics which illustrate the way sales have risen for her clients.

Terri's personal presentation style is smooth and free of distracting behaviors. This wasn't always the case. Years ago, she had to work hard to break the habit of saying "um" prior to making each important point in her sales presentations. Now she is well practiced in using her tools, speaking clearly, and pacing her presentation to maintain her audience's interest.

Two years ago, Terri decided to structure her sales presentations in this manner. And today, her audience is clearly participating in a presentation which is well organized, with ideas and concepts following logically from one to another. Terri's presentation fosters interaction throughout. She directs questions and comments to members of the audience and has structured her time to allow for fifteen minutes of questions and answers following the body of her sales presentation. Terri's presentation strikes a positive chord with all eleven prospects.

Earlier in the day, Terri's audience had taken another presentation from one of Terri's competitors. While his facts and information had been well researched and insightful, his presentation had not excited or involved them the way Terri's had. Now they would compare Terri's proposed budgets with her competitor's and spend several weeks evaluating the merits and costs of the proposed programs, weighing them carefully against their other options. During this period, Terri's comprehensive leave-behind will also stand her in good stead, and she looks forward to a favorable response.

Hunter C., the landscape architect introduced in Chapter 4, is presenting seminars in three cities in conjunction with a national horticultural association. The seminars are for advanced-level home and estate gardeners who wish to learn more about using water features in naturalistic landscaping. These seminars provide Hunter the opportunity to talk to potential clients nationwide while demonstrating his expertise in a topic of growing interest to more affluent home gardeners. Today, nearly 250 home gardeners have paid to attend the day-long seminar, of which Hunter is allotted one hour and thirty minutes.

Hunter's topic is in his own area of specialization. He has spent years researching and applying his knowledge in naturalistic landscaping. And water features—ponds, pools, and fountains—are among his favorite projects. As today's audience is comprised of fairly affluent, mid-level to advanced gardeners, his focus is on design and plant materials, not hands-on construction. In this way, he feels confident the content of his seminar will be relevant to the needs and interests of his audience.

Within his allotted time, Hunter must structure his presentation to allow for in-depth discussion of key topics without becoming boring. Today's presentation in New York will be formatted just like last week's in Washington, D.C. It is broken down into four sections. First, Hunter presents an overview of the various types of water features, followed immediately by a section concerning fountains. Next, Hunter takes questions from the audience concerning design and selection of plant materials to complement a variety of architectural styles. The remaining two sections on swimming pools and ponds are also followed by question-and-answer periods. This presentation structure fosters interaction and prevents what might be a technical and complicated seminar from becoming dull or esoteric.

Like several of today's presenters, Hunter has chosen to use slides to appropriately illustrate his seminar. The slides are projected onto a large screen at the rear of the stage. While the slides represent a capital investment—they were beautifully shot by a professional photographer expert in outdoor landscape work—Hunter will use them in many ways over the coming years. In addition to slides of public gardens, many feature projects of Hunter's own creation and allow him to offer case histories which cast him as an expert. The slide presentation is visually appealing and never dull.

Hunter's presentation style is, like Terri's, free of negative behaviors. A podium has been provided for his use, but he resists the temptation to huddle behind it. When fielding audience questions, Hunter moves comfortably about the stage and makes certain to ask the technician to raise the lights following each segment of slides. This "wakes up" the audience and allows him to make eye contact with the individuals who pose questions. This New York audience responds favorably to Hunter, asking thoughtful questions right up to the moment when he must yield the stage to the next speaker.

The attractive program created by the seminar's organizers contains biographical information about Hunter, a description of his company and its services and, most important, a telephone number for future contact.

Group Presentation Checklist

To prepare for your next important presentation, carefully review the following checklist. It asks simple questions relating to content, structure, and style. All your answers should be yes! If not, you still have some work to do.

Content

- Is the topic fully researched?
- Do you thoroughly address the subject?
- Is the content benefits oriented, detailing not only how to do something, but why?
- Is the content relevant to the audience's needs?
- If a sales presentation, do you propose relevant solutions?

Structure

- Are the ideas and concepts well organized?
- Does the presentation flow logically?
- Does the format foster interaction?

Style

- Is the choice of tools appropriate to the topic?
- Is the presentation visually appealing, never dull?
- Is your own presentation free of negative behaviors?
- Will the information be clearly communicated?

Tips for Polishing Your Presentation Skills

No matter what the type of presentation, your skill as a presenter will have a great impact on your overall success or failure. It's important to polish your physical and vocal skills and to eliminate any negative behaviors. To do this, set up a home video recorder on a tripod and make your presentation as if you were presenting to prospects or a seminar audience. If you don't own a video system, rent or borrow one and take a critical look at your performance.

Don't bother trying to practice in front of a mirror. It's simply too distracting. With videotape, you can just set up the camera and imagine yourself in front of your audience. That way you will have a true picture of your personal performance as it might appear to prospects. Review the tapes, work on your performance, and tape again. Consider asking someone whose opinion you trust to join you in appraising your performance. Here's what to look for:

EYE CONTACT. Speak directly to your prospects or audience members, moving your eyes around the room to make contact with specific individuals. This will help keep the audience focused on you.

CLEAR SPEECH. Mumbling, speaking in broken sentences, breaking off in the middle of phrases, speaking too softly, or speaking when turned away from the audience are all negative behaviors. Speak clearly so that the person in the farthest seat can hear you. If this is difficult to do without shouting, get a microphone.

ABSENCE OF ANNOYING/DISTRACTING MANNERISMS. Even the smallest personal habits can be magnified when in front of an audience. Mannerisms such as hair twisting, excessive hand gestures, pacing, or frequently using words like "um," "well," and "okay" must be eliminated.

GOOD PACING. Speech which is either too fast or too slow can be annoying. Pace your presentation carefully, speaking at a normal rate, neither racing ahead nor taking exaggerated pauses.

MODERATED PITCH. During normal conversation, your vocal pitch goes up and down, raising or lowering at the beginning or end of sentences. If you have a tendency to speak in monotones, practice moderating your pitch in order to maintain your audience's interest.

Natural and animated body movement. Avoid standing stiffly and unmoving with a poker face in front of your audience. If self-consciousness makes you stiffen up, try to focus your attention entirely on what you have to say and forget you even have a body. Speak and move naturally as you would in normal conversation.

No signs of nervousness. It's natural to be nervous when in front of an audience or making an important presentation to key prospects. While you may not be able to eliminate the nervousness, you can work to free yourself of the telltale signs. Obvious ones are shaking, twitching, stuttering, giggling, grimacing, breathlessness, and hurried or jerky mannerisms.

Handle materials well. Practice using your presentation tools over and over until moving them about is second nature to you. Rehearsal is essential to smooth handling of materials and it will pay off for you in the long run.

Draw in the audience and invite comment. Stepping beyond the prepared script makes many presenters nervous, but in most cases it's essential to building rapport. Know exactly at what points in your presentation you will invite comment, and anticipate questions and rehearse answers. While you cannot anticipate every contingency, planning and rehearsal will help you build the confidence necessary to handle these situations effectively.

Generally likable personality. While no one expects you to tell jokes like a stand-up comedian or smile continuously throughout your presentation, a stern poker face can alienate an audience. Some people frown or grimace when in deep concentration or to compensate for nervousness. Remember to relax, smile occasionally, and your natural "niceness" will come through.

APPROPRIATE APPEARANCE. Dress and grooming are important when in front of a prospect group or seminar audience. Examine your image on the videotape and think about the ways it might be improved. Fit your appearance to the audience and the situation. You will know what's appropriate. Extraordinary people sometimes cultivate an extraordinary appearance or image. If you're another Albert Einstein, that's probably okay. If not, you may wish to think of ways you can polish your personal appearance.

Five Guidelines for Producing Presentation Tools

There are five important considerations when selecting the type of tools you will use to sell your company, its products or services:

- quality
- cost
- value
- environment
- competition

Quality is, of course, always the first consideration. No matter what type of tools you choose to produce, they must be professional in appearance in order to reflect your company's quality image. Unless you are experienced in graphic design, video production, or an expert in photography, for example, it's best to utilize the services of professionals when creating presentation material. A sales presentation, in particular, is your time to shine, to pull out all the stops, and to make every effort to stand out as superior to the competition. Professional, high-quality tools and materials are essential here. Don't leave home without them.

For all small businesses, and home-based businesses in particular, the cost of quality tools is often an overriding consideration. Videotape production, for example, can be costly and always requires professional production. Yet it may be affordable to you if, as in Terri's retail sales consultancy, the videotape is shot in the normal course of your work. In Terri's case, videotape is often used to record focus groups or training sessions. For a nominal cost, she simply has the materials edited, adding a voiceover and music, into a cohesive story which forms a significant part of her sales presentation.

Select only the types of tools you can produce well within your established budget. Never attempt to produce extensive video or multimedia presentations cheaply. By cutting corners on quality or professionalism, the final product will undoubtedly look cheap. It's best to use less expensive tools such as slides or presentation boards and to execute them beautifully. Of course, the value of your presentation tools will be enhanced through repeated use. It may be valid to spend several thousand dollars on production of slides when you plan to use them over and over in different configurations for a variety of presentations. Also, a high-cost presentation, even when used once, may represent significant value if it helps you gain a prodigious piece of business.

Consider the environment in which your presentation will function. In what size or type of room will you be presenting? How many prospects or how large an audience will you address? What kind of technology will be effective in these environments? Small rooms and audiences allow for a more personal, interactive approach. They also require less presentation equipment such as video monitors and large projection screens. Conversely, tools such as presentation boards and flip charts are unworkable when addressing larger audiences. So fit your tools and materials to the environment you normally encounter when making group presentations.

Competition remains an important factor, particularly in a competitive bid situation. But never make the mistake of assuming, because your chief competition is presenting with certain types of tools or materials, that you must match them in your approach. For example, if you are competing against two other companies known to use slides for group presentations, then you may choose not to use slides for your presentation in order to stand out. Choose an innovative approach, using other tools or materials which make a strong impact. Your presentation may well be the one that is remembered as standing apart from the competition.

From Easels to Videotape: How To Choose the Right Medium

There is a wide variety of presentation tools from which to choose, ranging from a blank pad and easel through multimedia technology run with the aid of a computer.

Blank Pad and Easel

You will recall, management consultant Warren D. uses a blank pad and easel to present examples with figures which illustrate the advantages of working with his firm. This highly interactive method of presentation is most effective with small groups. The presentation itself must be extremely well planned or scripted and rehearsed so as to appear spontaneous. This requires a presenter who is an expert communicator. The advantage of presenting with a blank pad suspended from an easel is to lend an immediacy to the presentation. It may allow you to demonstrate solutions and show the process. This type of presentation is only appropriate in small, less formal environments.

Presentation Boards

An easel and professionally produced presentation boards are also excellent for use with small groups. The individual boards may be passed around for closer viewing, items may be removed or detached and examined, and the presentation itself can be easily reorganized. Cynthia and Alex S. use presentation boards to pitch their public relations services. They demonstrate case histories, show magazine covers, reprints, press kits, brochures, and specialties, and use the boards to outline their steps to reaching a customized solution for their prospects.

If you choose to work with presentation boards, they should be clean and attractive. Use black, gray, or another neutral tone to form an effective background for color materials. Your presentation boards must be prepared by a professional graphic artist or paste-up person. Text should be typeset and statted up or printed on a laser printer in a large point size. The typeface should be kept consistent and it should be dense, without a multitude of thin lines to interfere with readability. And, of course, text should be kept to a minimum.

Slides

Judy K. uses slides to present her line to jewelry store managers, buyers, and assistant buyers. Photo layouts of her fine gold and gemstone jewelry have been exquisitely captured by a professional photographer. Models are strikingly featured in some of the shots. Slides with color graphics depict successful sales results achieved by those stores carrying Judy's jewelry.

Like Judy, when your product has high visual appeal, slides can show it off to great advantage. Photographs can make use of special lighting, props, scenery, and even models, yet have a "real" quality which allows you to show product applications believably.

All slide shows should be professionally photographed. Even when presenting photographs depicting his own projects, Hunter is careful to rely on those landscape shots which have been professionally set and/or produced. And the text created to accompany your visuals must be scripted and well rehearsed. Of course, your slide presentation may be easily reorganized and used over and over again. Slides, however, do take the visual focus off the presenter, and lowered lights can put people to sleep before too long.

If you intend to use slides to present to small groups, an all-in-one projection unit resembling a small TV monitor can be purchased affordably. For larger groups, the standard screen and projection units must either be purchased or rented.

Transparencies (Viewgraphs)

Many presenters like to use transparencies or viewgraphs, particularly when the presentation or seminar must be organized on short notice. It's true these materials are inexpensive and easy to produce, but the result is often a dull presentation, generally only one- or two-color, with text or graphs. As projection equipment usually must stand in the middle of the room, viewgraphs or transparencies have to be changed by an assistant or the presenter must stand out in the audience facing the screen. Strong consideration should be given to other options before viewgraphs or transparencies are relied on for important presentations.

Videotape

Videotape appeals to all age groups. It is excellent for telling a story and relating emotion. Video can demonstrate benefits, show product and applications, show how a service is performed, or educate. Like slides, however, video takes the focus entirely off the presenter. Videos cannot easily be revised, and they must be professionally produced.

Thanks to the sophistication of today's audiences, video production must be well executed.

Use of videotape requires rental or purchase of portable equipment for small groups. Presentation to a large group may require multiple monitors or a giant-sized, rear-screen projection unit, sometimes found in more advanced conference facilities.

Leisha E. uses videotape to present at seminars or conferences, such as regional association meetings of gift and specialty store owners. Her presentation focuses on the growth of the maternity products market among baby boomers, yet allows her to present the advantages of carrying her maternity products in one's chain or specialty store. In her video, Leisha shows attractive in-store displays of her maternity products as well as sequences of pregnant mothers using the pillows which constitute the main portion of her line. A later sequence in the videotape shows lighted store signs and front windows of the many well-stocked shops carrying her products. While educating her audiences to the advantages of selling to this target market, she also takes the opportunity to demonstrate the benefits of carrying her product line, demonstrate the product itself, and show the ways others are reaping the rewards of selling her products.

Computer-Guided Multimedia Presentations

Certainly one of the most costly types of presentation tools is the multimedia presentation run or guided by a computer system. Generally out of reach for the home-based business owner, such systems require a large capital investment in equipment but do make an excellent presentation incorporating film or videotape, graphics, and sound. If yours is a high-technology business, particularly one associated with or a part of the computer industry, you may wish to consider this type of investment. Indeed, prices for such systems are always coming down as the technology evolves and becomes more available to a variety of purchasers.

Eight-Point Checklist for Selecting Presentation Tools

Here are the eight most important factors to consider before choosing the tools for your next presentation. Quality, of course, is always the principal factor. Select only those tools and materials which support the top-quality image you have created for your company, its products or services.

    1. Presentation environment. Will the room be large or small? Bright or dark? Use of videotape in a large room requires numerous monitors, yet it is preferable to using a pad and easel which would be nearly invisible at the front of an auditorium.

    2. Audience size. Will you be presenting to one or to two individuals or to one hundred? Some tools, such as slides, may be used with both large and small audiences, while many others may not.

    3. Level of formality. Is this a small, get-acquainted meeting or a dog and pony show? A group expecting an informal exchange of ideas and information will be put off by a formal presentation which requires them to sit passively and listen.

    4. Content. Will your presentation require sharing samples, or demonstrating complex facts and processes? Presentation boards lend themselves well to presenting printed samples. Videotape, on the other hand, can be used to teach complex concepts and impart detailed information in a way that is both entertaining and informative.

    5. Competition. In a competitive bid situation, what types of tools will your competition be using? What is their style of presentation? How many presenters will be involved? Rather than attempt to duplicate your competitors' expected performances, search for a method of presentation which helps position your firm as the unique solution.

6. Presentation skills. Are you a spontaneous, well-practiced, and expert presenter? Do you rely heavily on traditional presentation methods and carefully scripted and rehearsed presentations? Select a presentation method which helps you to shine. Avoid tools and methods that make you feel clumsy or unskilled—until you have had the opportunity to practice and build your expertise.

7. Long term value. Will the tools you prepare for your next presentation be used just once or will you be able to reuse them? Can you adapt them for use with a variety of prospects or in several seminars? If so, even relatively costly tools may prove to be valuable assets to your successful, long-term sales effort.

8. Cost. Can you produce a top-quality presentation within your budget with the types of tools you have selected? With tight budget constraints, its best to use knowledge, innovation, and imagination along with affordable tools to create winning presentations.

The success of your entire sales program may at critical times rest on your ability to make presentations which successfully sell your product or service. You have established a new business program, made the calls, used marketing communications, gotten the appointments, and fought for your right to present your capabilities to your target audience or prospects. Now it's up to you to focus all your energies and talents on assembling and executing presentations that win the business you and your company deserve.

chapter six

Building Your Company Image Without Breaking the Bank

Regina W. is president of a home-based business specializing in distinctive business events and conferences. Together with her part-time assistant and a network of independent contractors, Regina plans and executes business meetings, from luncheons for thirty and black-tie events for twelve hundred, to seven-day business conferences at exotic sites.

In the eleven years prior to founding her company, Regina earned her stripes by learning every aspect of the business. Fresh out of school, she worked for a short while at a travel agency, then moved to a Fortune 500 corporation where, in just a few short years, she became head of all meeting and conference planning. Later, she accepted a vice presidency at a mid-sized marketing communications company, where she planned and executed special events for a wide range of clients. Within several years, Regina had become responsible for everything from grand openings to incentive cruises. And she felt fully prepared to open her own firm specializing in event and conference planning.

During her first six months of operation, Regina's contacts and new business efforts yielded some positive results—predominantly small meetings and luncheons—but not the plum jobs her talents and background warranted. Not surprisingly, Regina experienced the same difficulties as countless other home-based business owners. Clients were willing to award her company the smaller, less risky contracts. But when it came to large, costly events or programs, they tended to select larger out-of-home–based competitors whose images projected experience and stability. In truth, Regina's competitors often had no more experience than she, and in the largest firms, the bulk of the work was actually performed by entry-level personnel.

After careful deliberation, Regina determined the best way to grow her business would be to invest in a family of quality tools which would create an image of strength and help position her company as expert in handling a full range of events, large to small. Only then could her company hope to compete toe-to-toe with the larger competitors for the plum jobs.

Like Regina, millions of Americans are happily going to work every day at home. As a home-based business owner, you have all the benefits and responsibilities of running a small business without the commute or high overhead of an out-of-home office. Unfortunately, many of your prospects and customers or clients still hold on to some negative stereotypes of home-based businesses—thinking of them as part-time or temporary employment, makeshift operations run from the kitchen table or in some way not "real" businesses. The best way for a home-based business owner to counter these misperceptions is to overcome them right from the start with a cohesive family of materials which work together to create a powerful company image.

Everything you create, from brochures and stationery to price lists or product sell sheets, must be integrated. They must work together as components of your company identity package. You would never call on a new business prospect wearing unmatched business attire, such as a blue pinstriped jacket with brown flannel trousers from another suit. The overall impression created would be jarring and, at the very least, unfavorable. For home-based businesses, company literature often must function as an outside salesforce and help to reduce the cost of personal selling. With a limited number of hours to expend in new business meetings, your sales support or company literature will be sent out to "call on" prospects, oftentimes prior to your meetings with them.

As a group, your cohesive family of sales tools must sell for you by communicating the benefits of working with your firm. A familiar analogy in selling is that of temperature: You make "warm" or "cold" calls to "hot" prospects. In one way or another, each communications tool attempts to change potential customers from a "cold" state, where they know nothing about your company, product or service, to a "hot" state, where they are prepared to make a buying decision. Sales support tools and marketing communications, such as direct mail, are responsible for raising the temperature initially, with personal selling adding the final "heat" to close the sale. The prospecting literature which comprises a part of your family of materials will fill the gap between advertising and personal selling and add as much heat as possible.

Since personal selling is always the most expensive means for adding heat, communicating with prospects via top-quality literature will move them closer to a buying decision while lowering your overall cost of selling. So, the dollars expended on production of top-quality tools and materials are an investment critical to your company's growth and long-term success in securing the most desirable clients or customers.

For Regina, the development of a powerful and effective company image would mean the difference between handling small luncheons and planning and managing gala dinners or major corporate conferences. In order to grow the type of business she wanted to own, Regina contracted with an expert creative copy and design team experienced in taking an integrated approach to materials development.

With their help, she created a family of materials including company identity, sales support, and marketing communications tools. Working together, the materials establish a powerful visual identity and communicate motivational, benefits-oriented messages to prospects.

Three Goals for Image-Building Company Literature

As you begin formulation of your own image-building tools and materials, consider how they will meet the three most important goals:

- to create a consistent visual image
- build awareness and establish your product or service as superior, and
- move prospects closer to a buying decision.

Creating a Consistent Visual Image

Each time a prospect is exposed to your corporate literature, sales support materials, and in some cases, your other marketing communications materials, the image conveyed should be consistent with that of the last piece of literature they saw. Making your image recognizable, distinct, clear, and consistent with the quality of your product or service is of paramount importance when developing your tools and materials.

In fact, a wide range of elements will comprise the visual image conveyed by your literature. The design style and format of the materials; choice of paper, typeface, and ink colors; line art, illustration, or photography; and even size and weight of the materials are component parts of your company's visual image. While the majority of these choices will be made with the help of professionals, ultimately your decisions must be guided by the nature of your company's prospects and the distinct image you wish to create.

For example, Warren D. and Terri L. are both business consultants. But that's where the similarity ends. Warren is a management consultant working with mid-sized corporations, many of them in manufacturing. Terri, a retail sales consultant, works with department and chain stores. Indeed, the differences in their consulting businesses, and in the types of prospects they target, have caused them to develop vastly different visual identities for their businesses.

Warren "dresses" his company literature in the same buttoned-down corporate look he himself carries. His company materials are printed in blues and burgundies on white or pale gray paper stocks. Typefaces are traditional serif types (the ones you commonly see with embellishments on the ends of the letters). And as a rule, his materials, even his direct marketing, are understated and visually "cool," relying on hard-hitting copy to turn up the heat.

Terri's materials target prospects in the fast-changing world of fashion, accessories, and home furnishings. These prospects expect a less traditional visual approach and respect a company whose visual image is consistent with their own up-to-date, fashionable sensibilities. Terri's materials must be contemporary yet warm, since her company's focus is on retraining store personnel to improve customer service. Her materials utilize a contemporary sans serif typeface, and warm, fashionable Southwestern colors on bright white coated paper stock. Sales support materials also rely heavily on the use of four-color photography depicting store personnel learning new skills and practicing them on the selling floor with customers.

Terri's direct marketing employs some of the creative flair retailers use to communicate with their own customers. In fact, her most successful mailer for opening doors to new prospect meetings is a large fold-over card whose top panel is die-cut in the shape of a clothes hanger. Copy induces prospects to reduce the number of clothes items hanging on the racks by improving customer service—all with the help of Terri's company. Even in this hard-sell direct marketing piece, Terri's company image is reinforced through consistent use of logo, sans serif typeface, contemporary design style, and Southwestern colors.

Both Warren and Terri have developed visual images unique to their own companies and through frequency, or repeated exposure, have created memorable and recognizable company identities.

Building Awareness and Establishing the Benefits of Your Product or Service as Superior

With the help of Chapter 1, you developed a sales and marketing communications platform from which all future messages would emanate. Prior to creating any company tools or materials, review your platform. Does it focus, not on what you have to sell, but on what your prospects want to buy? Does it identify a niche or specialty with which you can position against the competition?

To build awareness of your company's products or services as superior, your sales support and marketing communications materials must present a unified, benefit-oriented concept based on the target audience's needs. Company literature which promises to meet prospects' needs in a unique or superior way will be most successful in building awareness for your growing business.

Terri's prospects are department and chain store senior executives who hope to increase sales by improving customer service. The more quickly they can show a turnaround, the sooner they will stop losing money. Plus, the improvement in service must be long-range in order to keep customers coming back. Therefore, Terri has developed a program which meets their needs, promising, "Faster, longer-lasting impact on storewide sales and customer service." When detailing individual features, Terri promises to:

- "Develop programs to provide the service your customers want
- Make rapid, positive impact on storewide sales
- Ensure continuous improvement through post-training, in-store evaluation."

All of Terri's materials focus prospects' attention on these same benefits and features. From the smallest promotional tool to the leave-behind used to reinforce the impressions made in an important presentation, all materials underscore her company's principal message.

Moving Prospects Closer to a Buying Decision

Aside from your basic stationery package, the bulk of your sales support and marketing communications tools should play a significant role in the buying cycle. Create only those tools and materials which help move prospects to the next level—always a step closer to making a buying decision. All prospecting literature must motivate prospects to take action and close by providing a means to satisfy their needs, such as a toll-free telephone number.

For Terri, direct marketing tools are an essential component of her company's prospecting literature. Not only does her campaign create a consistent visual image and present the benefits of her company's services as superior to the competition, but her effective direct mail campaign also motivates prospects to take a sales presentation. Essentially, it transforms warm prospects on Terri's direct marketing list into hot prospects significantly closer to making buying decisions.

The corporate and association prospects Regina targets for her events and conference planning business can rely on her experience and worldwide contacts, her flair for innovation and unique events, and her attention to detail. In short, the benefits they expect include saving money on even exotic locales, looking good to their business associates, customers, or guests, and worry-free service.

To motivate prospects to contract for events which take advantage of her full range of capabilities, Regina has created three black-and-white brochure inserts which focus on exotic or luxurious locales for events and conferences. These inserts—reconfigured and run as a small-space, black-and-white ad series, as well—promise, "the extraordinary on an ordinary budget." Crisp, black-and-white photos are the principal visual elements. One insert (and ad) features a photograph of nine men and women seated around a mountaintop campfire surrounded by snowy peaks—not your typical setting for a strategy session. Another insert depicts a black-tie gala with couples dancing under the moonlight on the deck of a private cruise ship.

Regina relies on her experience and worldwide contacts to obtain the best rates and packages. In turn, her prospecting literature promises exotic or innovative events without extraordinary expense. This is substantiated by the visuals and corresponding headlines. Finally, to further motivate prospects to respond, an additional incentive is provided in the form of an offer to complete an event-planning worksheet which will demonstrate the prospect company's potential savings.

Both Terri and Regina have created company tools and materials which essentially move their prospects further along in the buying cycle. Like many home-based business owners, with limited time to expend with less-than-qualified prospects, the bulk of their tools and materials can function successfully on their own, without the added heat from personal selling.

Building your own company image will require a family of essential tools, sales support, and other marketing communications materials which carry consistent visual images and themes.

Tips for Producing a Family of Essential Tools

Begin by making a list of all the materials you will need to meet day-to-day business demands. Resist the temptation to rush off and quick-print stationery and business cards just to get started. Even these basic materials require forethought and planning, including decisions on logo, paper stocks, ink colors, typefaces, and other considerations, not the least of which is cost. It is simply less expensive to design, purchase paper, and print a family of materials together. This also helps to ensure color consistency and continuation of a visual identity which must be perpetuated throughout not only your essential tools, but also your sales support and many marketing communications materials.

The following is a laundry list of some general materials which often make up the essential tools for home-based businesses.

BUSINESS CARDS. Two-color business cards on coated stock look sharp and can coordinate with your entire family of tools. A coated white stock will absorb less ink, make your colors appear more brilliant, and look expensive yet cost just marginally more.

STATIONERY. Both standard and executive note-sized stationery should also be printed in two colors, like your business cards, on matching color paper stock. Opt for paper which is at least 25 percent cotton in flat (wove) or textured (laid) finish. The cotton content will add a richness and an "expensive" look to your stationery without adding significantly to the cost. If you create forms with the help of specialized computer software, you may wish to purchase continuous feed stationery for printing a variety of documents. Corresponding envelopes should have matching ink and paper for a complete look.

MAILING LABELS. Many materials, including 8½-by-11-inch brochures, proposals, and other tools, often require large mailing envelopes. Rather than incurring the additional cost of printing envelopes in a range of sizes, buy standard envelopes and order two-color mailing labels to match your cards and stationery. Your self-adhesive labels can be purchased in sheets for laser, inkjet, or impact printers and copiers or in rolls. Those in rolls generally tend to be smaller in size and may only have enough room for an address block. Sheet-fed, self-adhesive labels can be designed to accommodate your business return address plus a full-sized block for addressing. Attractive all white or airmail envelopes may then be purchased inexpensively at any office supply store. When customized with your two-color mailing label, they will correspond to and reinforce your company identity without the cost of printing on a wide range of envelope sizes.

CONTRACTS AND SERVICE AGREEMENTS. Oftentimes, businesses with large customer or client bases have preprinted contracts and agreements. These may be surprinted on standard two-color stationery or typeset and printed in two-color on a coated paper stock to match other materials, including business cards, brochures, price lists, sell sheets, and so forth.

COMPANY BROCHURE. While technically a part of your group of sales support materials, a company brochure is also an essential tool which few home-based businesses can afford to do without. If you are considering selling from a group of computer-printed pages and a three-ring binder or some other makeshift device, think again. Your company product or service brochure must work as hard as you do to position you against the competition and to convey the image of your company as strong and capable. In effect, your brochure must also act as your company representative when mailed to prospects and help you introduce your company in one-on-one sales presentations.

To decide upon the type of brochure you will need, examine the pieces used by your most successful competitors. Think of the many ways your brochure will work for you and the depth of information it must carry. Consider how its overall design will interface with that of the remainder of your tools and materials.

Select coated stock if photography or two-color images requiring tight registration will be used, and always when planning four-color materials. Thousands of beautiful uncoated stocks are, of course, available for one-color and many types of two-color printing jobs. Some, in fact, are quite expensive.

If this type of paper stock is your preference, then select a paper which coordinates with others to be used throughout your family of materials, just as you would when selecting a coated stock. But be prepared to lose some of the punch and upscale sparkle many of the coated stocks can give everyday materials like business cards and Rolodex cards.

The weight of the paper you select is important, too. You might choose to use a particular type of paper for your company brochure and related tools, varying the weight depending upon how each tool is to be used. Paper stocks, both text and cover, are available in a variety of weights (expressed in pounds) and thicknesses (measured in points). Work with your designer or printer to select stocks which are neither too flimsy for brochures nor so heavy they unnecessarily increase postage costs on direct mail, for example.

PRESS KITS. For many home-based businesses, advertising funds are limited and home-based business owners often rely on extensive public relations activities to build their company images. If this is your plan, consider how you will create a professional-looking press kit. Will any other type of tool, such as a company pocket folder or proposal cover, be workable to carry press materials? If not, now is the time to begin developing such an essential tool.

PRODUCT PACKAGING, LABELING, AND INSTRUCTIONS/SAFEGUARDS.   F o r some home-based businesses, the image created for the company's products will be more important than the image created for the company itself. In this case it is appropriate for the product to carry an identity all its own, and its image should reflect the nature of the target purchasers and their buying preferences. For example, a company with a new product to sell might develop an image for itself which is very corporate and buttoned-down, relying on cool blues and grays, in order to help obtain funding. At the same time, its product packaging might be orange and white, indicating the product is for purchase by everyone, people of all economic and social levels. Development of a new product identity and packaging can literally make or break the product's success. And product or image development should be entrusted only to highly qualified professionals.

Sales Tools and Letters That Increase New Business

Plan ahead to produce all the marketing communications tools and materials that will support your ongoing sales efforts. Consider how sales support materials will influence the way prospects and customers perceive your company—and how they will increase new business results and build sales.

ROLODEX®CARDS.   These are handy tools for building sales of business services which will be used on an as-needed basis. While carrying the same look and feel as your business cards, Rolodex cards carry more information. The tab should feature the type of service provided, such as typesetting, copywriting, or bookkeeping. Your telephone number should figure prominently, preferably centered on the card in a large type size. Key services and other important data should be listed (much as in a telephone directory ad). Rolodex cards keep your phone number handy when your customers need it most.

FOLD-OVER CARDS. Personal notes are an important means for following up with prospects and are indispensable tools to many in real estate and business services, among others. For home-based businesses and for any company with a finite budget, a generic fold-over card should be produced which coordinates with your company brochure, business card, stationery, and other materials. In fact, if paper stocks and inks match, you may be able to print your fold-over cards along with several of your other tools to maximize cost savings. Use an all-purpose design or message on the front panel and keep the interior blank so that your fold-over cards can be used as thank you notes, as business reminders, and in a wide variety of other circumstances. Have them printed, scored, and delivered flat to save as much as a few cents per piece on folding charges.

PRICE LISTS. For some types of businesses, presentation of a price list is an integral part of every prospect meeting. When used as a sales tool, your price list should coordinate with other sales support materials, including your company brochure. Ink colors, paper stock, type styles, and use of your company logo must coordinate with the rest of your family of tools. Take special care to have price lists typeset (or have them look typeset with desktop publishing) and printed to give the impression of your prices being firm or fixed. A computer generated price list on company stationery may look attractive, but give the unfortunate impression that your prices are less than permanent or are negotiable and subject to change.

But what if your prices do change with some frequency? How can you typeset and print materials without spending a fortune? That's easily accomplished by creating your price lists in two steps. First, have your price sheet designed, typeset, and printed in two or even four color. Include everything except the prices themselves, leaving a blank area for those to be surprinted later. Next, have your list of prices typeset in a format which you feel you can adapt over time as your prices change. Then surprint it, preferably in black, in small quantities on your preprinted price sheets.

SELL SHEETS/DATA SHEETS. These are used when a company has a variety of products or services which may be sold individually, or when upgrading or reintroducing a product or service. The sheets must coordinate with and ideally be incorporated into your company's brochure or principal presentation tool.

To accommodate sell sheets or data sheets, consider preparation of a company "brochure" which consists of a two-pocket folder, with the sheets functioning as principal inserts along with company data and background. Or consider a one-pocket folder which will accommodate company data on the front, inside left, and rear covers, plus data sheets and other inserts.

Plan for and design data sheets or sell sheets along with your sales and other essential tools, even if their actual production may be delayed. In this way you will avoid production of tools which appear mismatched. For example, a company which fails to plan ahead for data sheets and sell sheets may produce a company brochure which folds down to a #10 size. Then later, it might produce an 8½-by-11-inch sell sheet which, to be mailed along with the company brochure, must also be folded down to #10 size. This presents the prospect with two separate pieces of material which, after leaving the envelope, could easily become separated or lost. By planning ahead, the same company might have produced its brochure in a format which could readily accommodate later addition of product sell sheets for a unified, professional look—and a more effective sales presentation.

Adding photography to data sheets, for example, can alter the design requirements of your corporate brochure and overall family of tools. The use of four-color photography generally requires coated stock. In order to match your data sheets or sell sheets to other materials such as brochures, they too will have to be printed on coated paper. This is just one example of how planning and designing your family of tools as a unit, prior to development of any materials, can prevent costly mistakes down the line.

"STANDARD" SALES MEETING TOOLS. Review your family of sales support and essential tools to determine whether additional presentation materials will be required for normal, everyday meetings with prospects. When producing additional tools such as flip charts or even video presentations, be certain to carry through your corporate identity: colors, design style, logo treatments, and, most important, the benefit statements and key selling points drawn from your sales and marketing communications platform. In this way, all materials will reinforce your visual identity and convey a consistent, clear message.

PROPOSAL COVERS OR BINDERS. If your business is like the multitude of others which must provide written proposals to prospects, then proposal covers or binders will be among your company's most important image-building tools. Design and execution of these materials should take place along with preparation of your company's essential tools and sales support materials, never as an afterthought or as you are struggling to prepare a major proposal or presentation.

Regardless of whether this tool is to function as a leave-behind following a presentation or is to stand alone carrying your written bid or proposal, its look as well as its contents will significantly influence the way your prospects think of your company and its products or services. Unfortunately, young companies are often tempted to rely on generic, low-quality folders. This inevitably downgrades the quality of their presentation and proposal contents overall. It also detracts from the positive images they may have created with other materials and in one-on-one sales meetings and presentations.

Production and printing of these critical tools need not be expensive. One way to cut costs is to design a single cover sheet, perhaps picking up artwork which has been created for use elsewhere, such as on the cover of a corporate brochure. Print this sheet on a medium to heavy cover stock no smaller than 8½-inches-by-11-inches so that it can completely cover any letterhead or second sheets. This cover sheet can be used to customize standard three-ring binders with transparent vinyl front pockets. Simply slide in your top-quality cover sheet and you have a customized presentation tool or leave-behind. The cost will be much lower than if you custom printed your logo or company name directly on three-ring binders.

Or use your cover sheet when spiral-binding materials. Choose transparent vinyl front and back covers and a coordinating color spine, and insert your printed cover sheet in front of your stationery pages. The transparent vinyl covers will protect your two- or four-color printed cover sheet to make a polished impression. You need not own a machine or materials for spiral binding. Printers and others who supply copying services can often bind your proposals or leave-behinds in your choice of covers and spine colors for as little as a dollar or two per piece.

SALES LETTERS. Not to be confused with direct mail (a form of marketing communications sent to a prospect list in order to gain respondents or leads), sales letters are generally prepared on company letterhead and are used to follow up or, in some cases precede cold or warm calls. They are never mailed en masse but instead are directed to specific individuals whose needs have been at least preliminarily addressed. Produce a standard letter, or several, depending upon the variety of your prospects, and maintain them on disk. Then customize your letters to fit specific situations or prospect needs.

Sales letters will rely heavily on the salient points made in your sales and marketing communications platform, as do your company brochure and other sales materials. The content must always focus on the benefits the prospect is likely to derive by using your product or service. In other words, sales letters are outer directed, not inner directed; you will use "you" more often than "we."

Typically, a sales letter should be no more than a single page long. The letter may be accompanied by your corporate product or service brochure and other sales literature. Always address the prospect by his or her name—and be sure to get it right. Call ahead to the company's switchboard to verify the spelling and form of address—whether it is "Mr." or "Ms." ("Ms." is the proper form of address for a professional woman. Unless specifically directed otherwise, "Ms." is always correct.)

After the salutation, open with a reference to any previous contact or conversation, followed by a general benefit. In the body of your letter, resist the temptation to write about what "we do...we offer...we have," except as that relates to how what your company offers will be of significant benefit or use to the prospect. Remember, the prospect is reading with one question in mind: What's in it for me? Speak directly and succinctly to his needs, and you'll find your letter satisfactorily answers this question.

Close by proposing follow-up action. State clearly when you will call, confirm an appointment date, or mention any action you plan to take to move this relationship to the next step. If possible, close by summarizing your general benefit, much as you did in the opening. And sign the letter using your full name and title.

Two model sales letters follow. The first is an example of a sales letter management consultant Warren D. might use to follow up with a prospect with whom he has recently spoken (see p. 138).

The second example is a sales letter which could be used to follow up a cold call. In this case, Daryl R. is soliciting PC maintenance contracts from a computer retailer (see p. 139).

Following these parameters, create your own group of sales letters. Be certain they are outer directed and benefits-oriented. Remember to always answer the prospect's question, "What's in it for me?"

Dear Mr./Ms._____:

Thank you for taking time from your busy schedule to discuss your strategic planning needs and how we might work together to meet them.

Right now, increasing profitability is on the minds of business owners and executives across the nation. For the 1990s, the focus will not be simply on growing "bigger," but on growing "smarter" through effective strategic planning. With increasing pressure to get more out of every company dollar, most businesses, regardless of size, must maximize their return on investments in processes, equipment, and personnel. And that depends on quality senior-level planning up front.

Together, we'll analyze the strengths of your company's management systems and how the systems interface with product production, customer service, order tracking systems, level of computerization, your competition and position in the marketplace, and your long-range goals. Even a review of sales force management and systems can be included in this process. A step-by-step plan will quickly crystallize into creative long-range management strategies and tactics to meet your company's goals. Then, by working as an extension of your in-house staff, we'll facilitate implementation of top-flight management processes and programs.

The enclosed brochure will give you more important information about our firm. I'll telephone you in May, as you requested, to discuss further the many ways we can help your company achieve all its goals.

Sincerely,

Dear Mr./Ms. _____:

Thank you for taking time from your busy schedule to discuss the challenges you and your company face in providing profitable, top-quality PC maintenance to many of your most important customers.

Daryl's PC Maintenance's team of expert technicians provide dependable, round-the-clock service which can actually increase your company's sales. Plus, Daryl's PC Maintenance services cost significantly less than maintaining a comparable department in-house. And our current 30 day FREE TRIAL offer for up to ten PCs is an excellent, no risk way to save money while sampling our expert service.

Working with Daryl's PC Maintenance, businesses like yours have:

- significantly reduced in-house costs
- increased sales by offering additional value to customers, lowering purchase barriers, building customer retention and repeat sales
- plus, guaranteed customer satisfaction thanks to our 24 hour on-call program!

(Ending A) Enclosed you'll find more important information about our firm and how we can work together to increase your company's sales and your customers' satisfaction. I'll telephone you soon to set up a meeting at your convenience to discuss (I'm looking forward to our meeting on ____ at ____ and to discussing) the many ways Daryl's PC Maintenance can have a positive effect on your company's bottom line.

(Ending B) Enclosed you'll find more important information about Daryl's PC Maintenance. While you presently see no opportunities for us to work together, I'll keep in touch. And I look forward to demonstrating how our top-quality service can have a positive effect on your company's bottom line.

Sincerely,

How To Extend Your Company Image Into Marketing Communications Campaigns

ADVERTISING AND DIRECT MARKETING. For many companies, marketing communications campaigns are a principal means of educating a wide range of prospects to the benefits of their products or services. That's why, particularly in display advertising and direct mail, the image conveyed must be consistent with the image established in your family of essential tools and sales literature. These materials, and many of your other tools, will doubtlessly be professionally created. Designers and copywriters will rely on your sales and marketing communications platform for copy points. They will also carry through your logo design into these new materials, along with other elements of your company's "look."

Some changes are likely, however. For example, a three-stage direct mail campaign need not be printed in just your one or two corporate colors. Instead, a family of colors which will work in harmony with your other materials can be selected—that is, as long as the direct mail tools will be tailored to the same target audiences. If not, a color family should be selected which has the appropriate appeal to the target group for each mailing. Other elements, such as photography or illustration that did not appear in your corporate or sales literature, can be added to your advertising and direct mail materials.

Direct mail may also warrant a change in paper stock. For example, you might use a high-quality, matte-coated stock for your corporate brochure, but it would be inappropriate to use such a costly paper stock when mailing tens of thousands of pieces. In this case, a less costly coated stock, perhaps in a glossy or dull finish and of a lesser weight, might be more appropriate and save you money.

But beware: A designer or agency that brings you a radically different approach or look for your advertising or direct marketing materials might be more focused on creating interesting design than on creating a cohesive image for your firm. Be certain there are design elements in common and that the changes enhance your company's ability to create a lasting, positive impression which is consistent over time.

SLOGANS AND POSITIONING STATEMENTS. These are often improperly or poorly used. Slogans and positioning statements should be created by a professional copywriter as part of the process of formulating your corporate sales and marketing communications materials.

Positioning statements are inner-directed. They describe what your company is or does in just a few memorable words. Positioning statements often appear on letterhead and corporate brochures and under logos in business-to-business advertising. They're helpful in explaining a company's function when, for example, the name is obscure or does not directly describe the product or service the company provides.

Slogans, on the other hand, directly describe the benefit users will derive. They are commonly used as tag lines on commercials, such as Maxwell House's slogan, "Good to the last drop," and the slogan for Ford, "Where quality is job one."

For those who are not professional copywriters, it may be difficult to imagine the complexity and number of man-hours required to create effective slogans, such as the ones above. Many are subjected to rigorous research and testing prior to use. When considering the addition of a positioning statement or slogan to your sales and marketing communications materials, it's best to err on the side of caution. Frequently changing or upgrading your slogan or positioning statement will undermine your efforts to create a consistent image.

Once adopted, extend use of these and other elements of your corporate identity into trade show booths and materials, public relations releases, and all other marketing communications and promotional materials.

Twenty Tools for Company Growth

Building a successful and powerful company image depends on taking an integrated approach to materials development. This results in cost savings and ensures continuity in design and content of a bank of creative tools. Refer to the following list to select the tools and materials which will help your company reach its growth potential.

Essentials
- business cards
- stationery
- corresponding envelopes
- mailing labels
- forms, contracts, and service agreements
- company brochure
- press kits
- product packaging/labeling
- product instructions/ safeguards

Sales Support
- Rolodex® cards

- fold-over cards
- price lists
- sell/data sheets
- sales meeting tools
- proposal covers or binders
- sales letters on letterhead

Marketing Communications
- advertising
- direct mail
- PR releases on letterhead
- trade show booths/materials

Twelve Ways To Ensure a Powerful Image

After you have selected your group of tools and materials, you are ready to begin production. Work with your creative team and printer to be certain all the creative elements are consistent with the image you wish to project for your company, will appeal to your target audiences, and can be produced cost-effectively. The following twelve creative elements should be agreed upon prior to production of your company's image-building tools:

- paper stocks
- paper colors
- paper weights
- typefaces or typestyle
- ink colors
- design format
- logo treatment
- graphics
- positioning statement
- slogan
- photography
- illustration

When To Call in the Experts

Mike T. has been a successful real estate sales associate for over seventeen years. After choosing a real estate career, he worked for several years with a large national chain, then moved to a regional Washington, D.C.-area real estate company with multiple offices and a high-profile image. He spent a dozen years there and became one of the company's top sales associates, earning awards, recognition, and large commissions. At the same time, Mike continued his education in real estate, earning professional designations such as G.R.I. and eventually gaining his broker's license.

Once he became a broker, Mike had the professional credentials to manage one of his company's real estate offices. But this would have meant a significant loss of income, due to his employer's compensation structure. Mike's income would have dropped from the six-figure range down to about $40,000 per year.

While the loss of income was unthinkable, the concept of running his own real estate office looked more and more appealing to Mike. He decided, after long discussions with his wife and grown children, to open his own real estate firm—which he would manage and still maintain a high income. Instead of a storefront office, Mike decided to work out of his home office and "hire" sales associates who worked out of their homes as well. All were top agents who had well-equipped home offices and established customer bases. Like Mike, this group of successful sales associates had rarely used their companies' sales offices or relied, as beginning agents do, on walk-in or call-in traffic.

For Mike, the biggest problem after starting his business in this fashion would be giving up the company-supplied sales tools and marketing communications support. Indeed, during his first eight months in business, many of the challenges and difficulties Mike and his associates faced could be traced directly back to lack of effective tools and materials.

From the outset, Mike was overconfident in his ability to produce everything the company would need on his own, despite lack of any formal training or experience in copy, design, or production. With the help of an inexpensive desktop publishing software package, Mike created his company's logo, putting the name "Thomas Realty" in all capital letters and sans serif type.

When designing his company brochure, Mike found he was intrigued with the five or six choices of type available with his desktop program, so he chose three of his favorites and used them all. The copy was entirely features oriented, listing all of his personal qualifications and detailing the unique structure of his company, without translating those features into benefits or the advantages his target audience would realize when choosing to use his new company's services.

For direct mail tools, Mike created four flyers targeting homeowners who might be prepared to list their homes with his firm. Each had a simple graphic or clip art and a paragraph of copy about the services his company could provide to home sellers.

The stationery package was printed in two-color, including costly gold foil stamping of the company name. The brochure was printed in two-color as well, minus the foil, with black-and-white head-shot photos of Mike and each of his sales associates. The direct mail was printed in two-color, on 8½-inch-by-11-inch uncoated sheets folded down to #10 size to fit into standard envelopes.

Not surprisingly, all of Mike's materials were poorly received. His company name and logo in all capital letters and sans serif type, when translated to housing signage, became nearly impossible to read and had to be revised. But, since the stationery package had been printed with expensive foil stamping, the letterhead was not revised to match the more effective use of the company name in upper and lower case lettering on signage.

The brochure was disastrous. By mixing typefaces, Mike had created a brochure which appeared amateurish and unprofessional—exactly the opposite image he was attempting to create for his firm of top real estate professionals. The copy, solely devoted to features, was useless when it came to convincing home sellers to list with Mike's company. Plus, when two of his sales associates went elsewhere in the first four months, his brochure was instantly outdated, since it carried their photographs.

Direct mail, too, was a costly exercise in futility. The basic visuals were uninspiring. The uncoated sheets were a poor choice. They absorbed the heavy ink coverage making the colors appear muddy. But worse yet, without training in writing effective direct mail, Mike's pieces had no hook, motivating body copy, or strong call to action—a few of the important elements which can make or break the effectiveness of a direct mail package.

And now, eight months later, Mike is faced with an income significantly lower than he projected, all because he relied on poorly constructed sales and marketing communications materials which failed to create a positive image or increase and support sales for his new firm. All the sums expended in printing and postage might well have covered the expense he must now incur to engage the services of a design and copywriting team to construct a new family of sales and marketing communications materials. The team will enhance Mike's ability to use his desktop publishing program by creating design formats which he will follow when creating new materials, such as direct mail. They will recommend typefaces, paper stocks and ink colors. And they'll provide hard-working, professional copy for a full range of tools which Mike will produce—also on desktop—as needed.

Design, copywriting, advertising placement, and other related services are technical, highly specialized fields which take years of training and experience to master. Would you consider personally installing the electrical wiring in your new home an appropriate weekend project? Would you feel qualified to take apart and reassemble your car's electronic fuel injection system? As a home-based business owner, particularly in your first year, you must focus your energies on what you do best and rely on experts to provide services vital to your success and your company's long-term survival.

Key Interview Questions for Choosing the Best Creative and Media Talent

When selecting individuals or companies to provide creative services, you will have a number of options from which to choose. You need not select a big design firm or marketing communications agency out of the telephone directory to find highly experienced and expert creative talent. Many designers and copywriters have left major advertising agencies and design firms to become independent, forming creative teams as dictated by their clients' needs. Many are home-based. In fact, selecting independents or small creative firms may ensure you get first-string talent instead of the newcomers or trainees who might be assigned to your relatively small account at a larger firm.

Many of the new, small marketing communications companies specialize in taking a well-rounded, integrated approach to the creation of all tools and materials your company will use to address its target audiences, including advertising and public relations. Or you may choose to select a design firm or a design and copywriting team capable of doing everything but placing media. Design firms, provided they offer the depth of experience and qualifications you require, will offer a wide range of services. And independent designers and copywriters will generally have counterparts with whom they work on a team basis.

When interviewing any creative team, whether from an agency or design firm or as independent contractors, it's important to come prepared with your own presentation of information and background. Know your target audience and competition. Be prepared to outline the types of tools you'll need. Bring your sales and marketing communications platform and any written background materials. Also, bring along any tools and materials you particularly like, to give the creative team an idea of your own personal tastes and preferences.

And always come prepared with at least a preliminary budget. Never ask a creative team to tell you what the budget should be. Because there is such a thing as cost-effective design and production, the team will need to know whether they are building the Sistine Chapel or an abbey. It will be up to them to help you create a family of quality materials, not one item that includes lavish components at the expense of your other tools and materials.

Be certain to share all information with each creative team you interview, and prepare a list of questions to gauge their ability to meet your company's unique needs. Here is a general list to get you started:

Q: **How long/often have you worked together?** Select a team that has experience working together. They will have had numerous opportunities to work out their differences and streamline their working relationship.

Q: **What experience do you have in creating integrated materials or campaigns targeting audiences similar to mine?** The team you select must understand how to speak to your prospects. If your family of tools must address business audiences, consider only those creative teams experienced in business-to-business sales and marketing communications. When selling a product or service to consumers, select a team with a wealth of consumer sales support and marketing communications experience.

Q: **Are you experienced in my type of product or service?** To some degree, the creative team must be able to speak your language and understand what it is you have to sell. That doesn't mean they must be experienced in selling exactly the same product or service, but they must have met similar challenges. For example, a creative team which specializes in selling cars or clothing may not be familiar with the intricacies of selling technical products.

Q: **Can you share case histories which demonstrate how you have created a family of essential tools and extended the image into sales tools and marketing communications campaigns?** It may be difficult for the creative team you interview to demonstrate all of this with one case history. Clients often make the mistake of hiring a team to solve one part of the puzzle and then struggle with making the pieces fit. Those you interview may share several case histories in order to demonstrate the ways they can build a company image for you which can be successfully extended into the tools and materials your company requires.

Q: **Do you bill on a project or hourly basis, and what are your rates and terms?** Most designers and copywriters will provide you with a project estimate based on the number of hours they believe it will take to complete the work. Consequently, when one designer bids at an hourly rate significantly higher than that of his competitors, his overall project rate will look much higher. Also, expect many firms to have terms which include a large deposit, as much as 50 percent, prior to beginning work. Others may bill for work in progress or ask for the balance of payment on delivery.

Q: Do you have established relationships with typesetters, color separators, and printers? What is your markup on those "outside" services? It is important that your creative team handle all the technical aspects of production, working directly as your representative and providing guidance and technical specifications. Be certain the estimates you are given include the time to provide this valuable service or that the hours expended in technical liaison are covered by the markup they charge on these outside services. Ask, too, exactly what their company markup is. For some, 42 percent is an acceptable markup when buying printing on your behalf. If this is the case, you may choose to pay the printer directly and compensate your designer or creative director only for the time he or she spends in liaison.

Q: At what stages will I be called upon for input or approval? Under normal circumstances, there are numerous stages at which you should expect to be called on to approve materials. It's much less costly to make changes in the early stages. Be certain those creative teams you interview understand your wish to be an active participant in all phases of production.

If you require media placement, you may wish to interview marketing communications firms exclusively or a design and copy team for creative work and a media buying service for placement only. When interviewing such vendors, add questions which directly address the amount and type of media placed by the firm. Media costs (particularly broadcast rates) are often negotiable, and the more media one buys, the more negotiating power one has. Also, established relationships with media sales reps and special training and expertise in media planning and analysis should be among the attributes of the specialized vendors you select to place your media. Here are some sample questions:

Q: **Describe your process of media analysis and placement.** Media analysis is highly involved, almost scientific sounding in its description. In Chapter 7 you'll learn many of the basics of media planning and placement. The vendors you interview ought to be able to give you a simple overview which will provide insight into their depth of experience and knowledge.

Q: **What percentage of your firm's/agency's placements are in print advertising? What percentage are in radio? What percentage are in television?** The parameters of print and broadcast buying are vastly different. If you intend to use primarily business-to-business trade publications, look for a vendor with in-depth experience in print. If, on the other hand, you plan to engage in a spot television buy, you should select a vendor with some buying clout and experience in negotiating and purchasing spot television.

Q: **Describe how your company evaluates direct mail lists.** Business-to-business marketing communications companies should be experienced in negotiating for and purchasing direct mail lists from a variety of vendors nationwide. This is a highly specialized area. If you plan to rent local, regional, or national lists, you will wish to engage a firm with established relationships with list vendors and the depth of knowledge necessary to help you find the list that most narrowly targets your specialized audience.

Q: **Are you compensated by fee, media commissions, or both?** When budgets are small, media commissions may not cover the amount of time required to place your schedule. Under these circumstances, vendors may ask to be compensated additionally on a fee basis. It's important to negotiate this particular point before hiring any vendor for media placement.

As when hiring any support person or team, references are important. Design and copywriting teams should provide at least three client references. Media placement companies should provide client references and three media references as well.

Twelve Ways To Save Money on Quality Tools

By now you have all the necessary information to build a consistent visual image for your company, create materials which will build awareness, and establish your product or service as superior while moving your prospects closer to a buying decision. To help you maximize your company's investment in building a quality image, here are twelve ways to save money and avoid the common pitfalls of creative production and printing.

1. Design and copywrite all necessary materials together. This reduces the time charges from the creative team.

2. Print groups of materials that utilize the same colors and paper stocks together. This saves the printer setup time and reduces printing charges.

3. Print one large quantity instead of two small quantities of materials as needed. This will reduce your cost per piece.

4. When printing in more than one color, always request a blueline (a proof of your final camera-ready art printed in light blue). This will enable you to pick up any errors or items which must be changed prior to going to final printing. Changes at blueline cost money, but they are significantly less expensive than the cost of reprinting an entire piece.

5. Whenever possible, avoid expensive secondary processes such as foil stamping, embossing, and gluing of printed pieces.

6. Beware of the false economy of low-quality paper stocks. Never sacrifice your company's image for marginal savings.

7. Meet with a local postal representative to find ways of reducing your company's mailing costs through use of bulk mail or barcoding, for example.

8. Hire professionals to do things right the first time. They will set the parameters for logo, typeface, colors, paper families, the use of photography or illustration, and they will manufacture all your tools with the right components.

9. Maximize the savings of desktop publishing, but avoid the do-it-yourself pitfalls by using professionals to fill in the gaps in your knowledge or expertise.

10. Create materials which can do double duty. For example, create folders which hold both sales inserts and proposals. Use the same artwork for multiple materials. Revise and reprint ads as mailers or inserts.

11. For mailing larger pieces, use standard envelopes with custom-printed labels.

12. Create materials with a long shelf life. Your more expensive materials should be free of anything which will make them obsolete quickly. Maximize your investment in quality tools and materials by producing a family which will stand the test of time.

chapter seven

How to Plan, Select, and Place Media

When used properly, media vehicles will help you create an image for your company and generate qualified leads on a level virtually unattainable by any other means. In fact, because of limited time and staff, many home-based business owners must rely on use of the media more than their larger out-of-home–based competitors. Without advertising, public relations, or direct mail, you would have to personally sell to every member of your target prospect groups—and not once, but over and over again. Of course, this would be impossible. Yet many small business owners of all types shy away from using the media, often passing up the opportunity to address thousands of potential customers or clients because they are uncertain about the way the media work and their attendant costs.

Should you use newspapers or magazines, and which ones? How often must you advertise? When will PR do the trick? What is the single most cost-effective way of reaching your target audience? For most home-based business owners, whose small, conservative budgets dictate the most educated use of media dollars, answers to questions like these take on paramount importance. This chapter provides insight to the fundamentals of media usage to help you create marketing communications programs which stimulate business growth.

The Creative Process of Advertising

Advertising production is in reality a "manufacturing" process which is both highly technical and extremely specialized. As with any manufacturing process, the quality of the components and the way in which they are assembled determine the efficacy of the finished product. Because the key ingredient in this creative manufacturing process is people, they must be trained and experienced in performing their own specialized jobs. Designers, art directors, copywriters, creative directors, paste-up artists, production managers, traffic managers, account executives, and others may all work together on a single print ad to move it from the initial concept stage to publication-ready materials. At small agencies or design firms, these roles may be undertaken by fewer people who specialize in a greater number of areas, but the result is still the same.

Advertising looks easy because the final product reduces complex subjects to simple, emotion-based concepts which relate to basic needs. Over many years, the essential elements of every type of advertising have been identified and confirmed through extensive, never-ending research and testing. Not surprisingly, the essential elements of a successful ad vary depending upon the medium and the type of product or service being sold.

For example, print advertising for industrial products shares key component requirements with many types of consumer product advertising. Basic rules or guidelines for production of headlines and body copy and a call to action may apply in both cases. But visually, industrial product advertising most often relies on demonstration of the product or its applications. On the other hand, visuals which accompany consumer advertising generally depict the benefits or rewards of using the product. For an established consumer product like a refrigerator, for example, it's no longer necessary to demonstrate how or why a refrigerator works. Consumers simply assume that it does. Instead, the advertiser demonstrates how the special features of the new refrigerator will provide benefits to enhance the purchaser's lifestyle.

Advertising professionals, and many design professionals as well, are expert at assembling the essential elements for each medium. What gives the components life or spark is the creative treatment. It's the creative treatment or process which puts a compelling twist in the "tried and true," taking the audience through the "pitch" from a unique angle. And to be remembered for even a short span of time, an ad must fight hard to win the attention of readers, viewers, or listeners who are bombarded by thousands of advertising messages each day.

To be successful, an ad or series must be manufactured with all of its essential elements, have a creative spark or twist which is compelling, and, finally, be supplied to the media in a form which meets exact manufacturing specifications. This may involve a number of secondary processes, from screening black-and-white materials or color separating four-color subjects, to editing, mixing, and duping radio and TV spots.

In the end, the effectiveness of your overall media campaign will rely as much on the quality of its creative production as on media selection and scheduling. And while advertising production costs vary dramatically, the bulk of your dollars will, over the life of a media schedule, be expended in ad space and time. In essence, an ineffective ad can cost a fortune—while a well-produced ad can earn you one.

Rather than risk the success of your marketing communications campaign on a do-it-yourself effort, search for advertising production experts who are experienced in marketing your type of product or service to similar target audiences. Many have left some of the country's most successful agencies to start their own small, often home-based firms. Candidly discuss your budgets and needs. Select a firm that is capable of providing highly creative concepts, and can execute those concepts affordably while fulfilling all the elemental requirements of your chosen medium. Experience is critical here. Be certain to ask tough questions when interviewing, such as those outlined in the previous chapter.

How To Choose the Right Media Mix

To make the most of your marketing communications dollars, you must select those media which most narrowly target your unique audiences and which are well read and looked to as sources of information by them. Reexamine the target audience profile you developed according to the parameters outlined in Chapter 2. When buying media, a principal goal is to select those vehicles which reach the highest percentage of your target audience with the least amount of waste. Clearly, getting the best media buy is not the same thing as finding the cheapest ad. Sometimes buying the cheapest ad space is simply a means of guaranteeing you'll reach the fewest people. The best use of your media dollars is to buy a mix of media with enough frequency of exposure to reach and penetrate your target audiences.

To help you select those types of media which will target your specific prospect groups, here's a brief overview of each.

Newspaper

Your city or town's daily or weekly newspaper may be useful in reaching both consumer and business-to-business target audiences. But unless you sell your product or service to the bulk of the newspaper's circulation area, you may be paying a premium to reach many thousands of readers your company cannot serve. Major dailies, however, often offer zoned sections or editions which are delivered exclusively to subscribers and newsstands in designated geographic areas in order to provide advertisers with smaller market areas more efficient buys.

Generally divided into special-interest sections such as Business, Home, Weekend, and Sports, large dailies in particular offer something for everyone. By placing your advertising in the appropriate section, you should reach readers with a predisposition to or special interest in your message. Interior design services tend to advertise in the Home section and banks in the Business section, for example.

In this way, newspaper sections which regularly carry display advertising of a particular type become—like their classified counterparts—"search corridor" vehicles. That means these are places readers look to for information on products or services when they've made a decision to buy. Just as a newspaper reader might go through the Automotive classifieds when he or she has made a decision to buy a car, readers may also peruse the Business section on a given day of the week when banks use display advertising to promote their best rates. The reader who has already made a decision to obtain a home equity loan might scan this "search corridor" of financial display ads to select an institution offering the best rate. Search corridor media offer the best opportunity to reach prospects who are prepared to purchase what you have to sell.

In many cities, newspapers devoted entirely to business news offer business-to-business advertisers a means for reaching their target audiences with less waste than with a major metropolitan daily, which reaches consumers and businesses alike. Business newspapers are often weeklies with fewer total readers, ad pages, and correspondingly lower advertising costs. Prior to buying ad space, the audit statement should be reviewed to determine whether your specific target audience is a large enough percentage of the overall readership. If you target lawyers, for example, yet the bulk of a publication's readership is in the real estate business, you must select another business-to-business vehicle which more directly targets your prospect group.

Suburban newspapers take up where the major consumer dailies leave off. They focus on local and community news and generally fare best for local consumer advertisers. If you offer a consumer product or service, for example, which is available to a select geographic market covered by a successful suburban newspaper, this paper would represent a more efficient advertising buy—one with less waste—than buying the full circulation of a major metropolitan daily which serves a much wider geographic area.

Newspaper display advertising is generally sold in Standard Advertising Units (SAUs). But some smaller newspapers have not yet adopted the SAU system, and the exact specifications for each advertising unit will have to be obtained by you or your agency or design firm. Screen densities (dots per inch) will also vary by publication. Some may require a 65-line screen, a coarse screen with fewer lines per inch, and others 85 lines or more.

Classified advertising, unlike display advertising, is often "pub set." Newspapers will typeset your copy and make it camera-ready for you up to a certain size limit, as dictated by the specifications of each individual publication. However, if you have the option of running camera-ready art in the classified section, you may wish to do so. Use type in a larger point size and graphics to help your ad stand out on the page.

Mike T., the Realtor introduced in Chapter 6, uses a combination of classified listing ads in the Real Estate section of his city's daily newspaper and display advertising in other search corridor media to attract both buyers and sellers. Mike uses a special software program to help him produce full-page display ads for each prominent listing (a home listed by its sellers for sale by his company). His display ads are run in publications specifically targeting those who have made the decision to buy or sell a home. In addition to demonstrating the attributes of the property Mike is listing, he uses a portion of these display ads to relate the benefits of selecting his company. Mike places his own advertising because the media he relies on is non-commissionable (does not pay 15 percent to advertising agencies) and offers significant help in making his artwork camera-ready at no additional cost.

Kathleen M. relies on both the creative and media placement services of her agency to promote her growing interior design firm. Her media mix includes black-and-white advertising in the weekly Home section of her metropolitan area newspaper and a half-page, four-color island (which is surrounded by editorial) in the city magazine. Kathleen's newspaper ads run every week for at least six weeks in a row, both spring and summer, and creative execution is never changed until an ad has run at least several times.

The Home section is a highly competitive arena, with many advertisers promoting sales and price-sensitive offerings. But Kathleen's advertising focus is on her company's range of services. And she uses seasonal headlines which promote urgency rather than discounts which would cheapen her company's image. Magazine advertising is also seasonal, but the elegant creative execution focuses predominantly on the range of superior services her small firm offers.

Magazine

Like newspapers, magazines generally fall into the categories of consumer and business-to-business (trade) publications. Both are created to meet the special interests of their own particular group of readers, and there is a magazine for every type of interest under the sun. To begin narrowing down the range of publications which target your specific audience, your agency or buying service will generally start by examining the Standard Rate and Data Service (SRDS) directories which list publications by category. They will send for media kits of those publications described in the SRDS as most narrowly targeting your audience. And they will review publications to select a magazine or group of magazines which offer an appropriate advertising and editorial environment for your product or service.

Many home-based business owners, in particular those who are selling specialized services, may not wish to reach consumer or business audiences on a national level. They should consider regional editions of national magazines. When available, regional or demographic buys allow advertisers to target specific buyers, narrow geographic markets, or both.

An alternative for local advertisers are city-wide magazines generally published in major metropolitan markets. These publications are often consumer-oriented, but some are slick publications devoted entirely to the business of a city or large market area.

Magazines, although they may contain advertising of particular relevance to an area of special interest—such as fashion, cars, or anything from air pollution to flooring—they are not generally considered search corridor vehicles. That's the sole function of directories, as well as product tabloids which consist of advertising only.

Directories abound for virtually every product or service available to businesses. Consumers rely on directories like the Yellow Pages to fill their day-to-day information needs. Directories published by trade magazines have a longer shelf life than regular issues of the magazine itself and often make for excellent advertising opportunities. When choosing between several directories that reach the same audience, always select the ones your best prospects will use the most. Look for directories that do not charge for listings and, consequently, are extremely comprehensive and attract the largest number of advertisers.

Advertising display unit sizes are not uniform from one publication to the next, although they may be similar for all standard or all tabloid publications. Ad sizes are expressed in page increments such as one-quarter, one-third, one-half, two-thirds, and full-page sizes. Use of four-color materials can add a premium of as much as 35 percent or more to the cost of your ad, although this expense may be well warranted. Studies have shown over time that readership scores for four-color advertising may be as much as 45 percent higher than for black-and-white.

The black-and-white line screen for magazines is much finer than for newspapers, around 133 lines, and materials or veloxes must be made to tight specifications. Four-color materials typically must be supplied in the form of chromalins or progressive proofs and four-color negatives.

Many national, regional, and local consumer and trade publications offer classified advertising sections. Like newspaper classifieds, these are often pub set and, for some advertisers, offer an excellent opportunity to reach qualified target audiences with a minimal investment. Some trade publications offer photo plus copy classifieds. This popular ad format gains greater attention from readers. Plus, these ads often carry reader service numbers like display ads, but for a fraction of the cost.

Ginnie and Sam P., who sell rare potted herbs from their country nursery, rely on a well-targeted campaign in national magazines to build the mail order side of their business. After significant results from small classified ads placed in several painstakingly selected magazines targeting their affluent urban target audience, Ginnie and Sam interviewed and contracted the services of a well-known direct marketing agency. With their help, the couple launched a successful, small-space display advertising campaign in more than a half dozen upscale gourmet and home magazines. Their direct marketing agency also developed and tested unique packaging for their "three pot" sets, which proved highly appealing to the target audience which, by this point, had been analyzed down to the smallest detail. The product and packaging were then pictured or illustrated in the small-space display ads and described in the few remaining classified advertisements.

Regina W., who targets regional accounts for her events and conference planning business, chose the regional editions of national newsweekly magazines at key times of the year, based on advice from her full service advertising agency. While it appears to readers that Regina's company is advertising nationally in prominent weeklies, her company is paying only for the subscribers in her market area. This gives her company the appearance of strength and stability critical to her long-term success in handling major conferences and events worldwide. In addition to these regional buys, Regina's media mix includes small-space, black-and-white advertising in a prominent regional business magazine and advertising in special, editorially pertinent issues of a local area business newspaper.

Radio

Many home-based businesses, particularly when just starting out, are undercapitalized or are funded directly by their founders out of savings and other personal accounts. For this reason, radio advertising is often dismissed as too costly or impractical. But before dismissing radio as a media option for your home-based business, you should know that radio is one of the best vehicles available to you for target marketing within a local area. Radio stations themselves target very specific audiences through their formats and programming. Like magazines, there are radio stations with formats to suit virtually every type of audience. And the stations themselves, as well as various research and ratings bureaus, know exactly who their listeners are.

For example, of all the radio stations in your area, you should be able to determine exactly which ones have the highest number of listeners who fit your target audience profile both geographically and demographically. You can pinpoint the radio station with the highest number of listeners in your county or in surrounding counties who, for example, are female, aged 25 to 49, and who work outside the home. Or you might pinpoint the station that reaches the most working men over age 45 in afternoon drive time (3:00 P.M. to 7:00 P.M., when business commuters are returning home from work).

To sell a consumer product to all radio listeners fitting a specific profile, you might have to buy five or six stations with sufficient frequency to penetrate your audience—a costly enterprise. To reach narrower, more specialized audiences, however, may require purchase of a lengthy flight of spots on just one station in a fixed position, such as by sponsoring a daily news or weather segment on just one well-targeted radio station.

Lie Sun C. has been president for three years of a home-based bookkeeping and payroll services company, which she runs with the help of her sister-in-law partner, her college-aged daughter, and three full- to part-time bookkeepers. Thanks to full computerization, specialized software, and an efficient staff, Lie Sun's company handles payroll services for as many as twenty-five client businesses at any given time. In order to sustain this volume and continue to grow her successful company, Lie Sun's media mix includes black-and-white advertising in a weekly business newspaper and in a monthly city magazine whose readership includes a high percentage of small- to mid-size business owners.

Lie Sun's company also benefits from a steady stream of leads produced by judicious use of radio. She sponsors a special financial news segment in afternoon drive time on an all-news radio station whose listenership closely matches her company's target audience profile. Her spots, paired with opening and closing, ten second "billboard" announcements, run once per day in a fixed position (at a specific time) five days a week, three weeks straight. Then they are off the air for two weeks and back on again for another three-week flight. By contracting for five spots a week for a total of 18 weeks on the air, Lie Sun has obtained an excellent rate from the radio station and ensured enough frequency to create an awareness of her company's name and its services among this station's listenership.

Radio advertising costs are a function of ratings, supply and demand, the dayparts in which the spots will run, the total number of spots, and one's ability to negotiate well. Lie Sun's company employs a local advertising agency to create and place all media. Ken D., president of an 18-month-old executive travel service business, also uses an agency to place radio spot buys in three metropolitan markets. Ken tested his radio strategy in his local market, and when it proved successful, he expanded to two additional markets which his research and experience told him would yield the greatest opportunity for sales.

Ken began using radio when his agency recommended he sponsor a weather feature on his city's top-rated, adult contemporary station. To gauge the results of the test, they used a special incentive to build response rates quickly: promoting a special executive getaway package for two when one's company booked over a certain amount of travel. As leads came in by telephone, names were added to Ken's prospect database. Within ten days, all prospects were mailed special "kits" with information, details of the offer, and further inducement to book quickly to begin earning travel points right away.

After staffing up to support the new business activity and accounts, Ken authorized his agency to launch the same promotion in two additional cities—with one change. The success of the promotion enabled Ken and his growing company to buy additional spots on as many as three stations per market, allowing him to build momentum more quickly by penetrating his audience more thoroughly on a city-wide basis.

Television

Home-based business owners located in the smaller television markets may have a greater opportunity to use TV to market their products or services to local consumers or businesses. But for many who are located in major metropolitan areas, the cost of buying a schedule during quality programming targeting specific, large audiences and with enough frequency to penetrate makes television simply unaffordable.

For television, much like radio, cost is determined by individual program ratings, seasonality and the inventory of spots available (supply and demand), and a number of other factors, not the least of which is your agency's or buying service's ability to negotiate for a long-term purchase. Also like radio, you can target highly specific audiences with a well-researched spot buy across a number of television stations in a given market. Of course, simple analysis should reveal during exactly which programs and at what times of day you will most efficiently reach your target audience.

The cost for thirty seconds of TV airtime can range from hundreds to many thousands of dollars. Production costs, too, thanks to the sophistication of today's television viewing audience, can range from just several thousand dollars to hundreds of thousands of dollars for one TV spot. If you choose to use television and production costs are a concern, a simple visual concept beautifully executed is your best bet. On a modest budget, keep production values high and rely on creativity—not special effects, elaborate sets, or high-cost celebrities—to make your product or service shine.

Many television stations, including cable, offer advertisers low-cost production. Their production capabilities are usually confined to shooting on tape in the studio or on limited locations with minimal sets. Visually dull, low-end spots with poor production values are often the result. This type of production should be used only when it will not negatively impact the image you wish to convey for your product or service.

Low cable television rates in many parts of the country have begun to make the use of television more affordable for home-based business owners. But beware: Low cost may mean poor reach per spot. Cable stations still have fewer viewers and greater difficulty in providing exact numbers upon which to base a buying decision. The percentage of households wired for cable varies by market, and among those households with cable, it may be difficult to determine the number and makeup of the viewing audience for a given cable program. And for many home-based business owners, the significant costs associated with television production outweigh the positive benefits of lower media costs for a more speculative cable TV spot buy alone. However, if you are producing TV spots to run on a wide variety of stations, then adding cable stations to your mix may enhance the reach of your spot schedule for a modest additional cost.

Leisha E. has used direct response television advertising to build sales of her maternity pillows nationwide. Leisha first expanded sales of her maternity pillows and related products from beyond her local market by using small-space, black-and-white "shopper" ads in national publications whose readership is comprised primarily of women of child-bearing age. As sales grew and Leisha's company expanded, she contracted with a national media buying service to test direct response advertising in those markets which were generating the greatest number of leads from the ongoing print advertising.

Like many direct response spots, Leisha's thirty-second TV commercial was produced on videotape by a local production company, featured the benefits of the product, demonstrated the product in use, and provided a toll free number for credit card orders. The test in several markets produced dramatic results, and Leisha authorized her buying service to negotiate for and place spot schedules on a market-by-market basis in key cities nationwide. Many of the spot schedules concentrate on non-prime-time programming on strong, independent television stations in order to avoid the high cost of prime-time network programming. TV spot response rates are closely monitored and schedules are continually fine-tuned in order to maintain response rates at levels which have been predetermined as satisfactory.

Direct Mail

At one point or another, the medium the majority of home-based business owners are most likely to use is direct mail. Their success will hinge as much on the quality of their lists as on effective creative execution. The creative manufacture of direct mail packages requires specialized knowledge and expertise, as does list buying. List buying is actually a misnomer; list renting would be a more appropriate term, since most lists are rented and supplied on magnetic tape or labels for one-time use only. National list houses abound. Some offer exclusively consumer lists, others specialize in business lists, and many trade publications rent subscriber lists.

The cost of list rental will range from a base rate perhaps as low as $25 per thousand for a general consumer list by zip code, up to $80 or as high as $200 per thousand for specialized lists with many qualifiers. Use of an exclusive list may cost up to $2 per record. For example, a list of all homeowners in a set of zip codes would be fairly inexpensive to acquire. But add qualifiers, or "selects," such as all homeowners who have been in residence at least five years and have two or more children, and you can increase the cost to rent such a list substantially. Also, list sources will often require a copy of your mailing piece before releasing their lists.

Many marketing communications and direct marketing agencies, most media buying services, and some advertising agencies are skilled in list buying. If you are handling your media directly and need assistance in locating the best qualified list for your special purposes, consider using a list broker. On your behalf, they will contact sources all over the country to identify lists which meet your parameters. They will help you select a list vendor which offers at least marginal guarantees and well-cleaned, well-maintained lists provided in the format required by your mailing house. Most list companies pay a twenty percent commission to recognized brokers. That is, a broker is charged twenty percent less for the list and in turn marks it up 20 percent when billing you. Essentially you pay the same price as if you were to purchase the list directly.

In addition to the quality of the list, other factors, especially mailing frequency and mailing dates, can affect the outcome of your direct mail campaign. Often, it's necessary to mail three or more times to the same list to achieve the optimum response levels. If you plan multiple mailings within a several month period, be certain to buy duplicate sets of labels when you order your mailing list. Dupe lists may cost 50 percent or less than the cost of the original, but all sets of labels must be ordered together in order to achieve this savings.

As a general rule, most list companies clean and update their lists at least annually. So check on when the next update is scheduled before ordering duplicate lists for multiple mailings. And never order duplicates for mailings scheduled more than three or four months in the future, or postal carrier route changes may necessitate using a service bureau to "clean" the addresses.

Also, be certain to mail in sufficient quantity to produce the numbers of leads or sales required. For example, typical direct mail response rates may be as low as 1 percent to 5 percent, although some extremely proficient practitioners glean response rates of 10 percent or better.

Mark B., president of the home-based accounting company catering to small and mid-size businesses introduced in Chapter 1, uses direct mail to build his prospect list. Soon after opening his business, Mark rented a mailing list (with the presidents' names) of all businesses in a given size, by industry, in his market area. All those who responded to his accounting offer were added to his prospect list and received a follow-up warm call.

Regina W. also uses direct mail to build prospect lists for her events and conference planning company. Instead of using a list broker as Mark does, Regina relies on her full-service agency to negotiate for and acquire a regional mailing list of businesses with over a given number of employees or sales personnel. Like Mark, Regina mails directly to the company presidents.

Most mailing lists are for that purpose only; they are not to be used for telemarketing. When telephone numbers are required, you may pay a substantial premium, and many lists are simply unavailable for any telemarketing purposes whatsoever. But once a lead is generated by your direct mail, you are free to contact your new prospect in any way you like.

In addition to the quality of your list and creative package, timing is critical to the success of a direct mail program. Depending upon your product or service and to whom you are selling, there are in fact certain months of the year which have been, through research, proven to be the most successful. December is a good month for financial direct mail, for example. To determine what your best times of year might be for successful direct mail marketing, consult with your agency or contact the Direct Marketing Association.

Weighing the Costs When Buying Space and Time

When buying media, your principal goal must always be to obtain the best buys for your media dollars. In general, costs are based on the projected number of readers, listeners, or viewers who will be exposed to your message. But other considerations influence cost as well.

If, for example, you have targeted an audience which is highly specific, unique, or difficult to reach by any means other than one or two trade publications, you may expect to pay a premium for ad space. This will normally be the case when trying to penetrate a particular business or professional group which reads only select publications. In broadcast, no matter what the ratings, supply and demand will affect spot cost. During periods when there is less demand by advertisers for airtime, it is often possible to negotiate lower spot costs.

Although virtually all broadcast rates are negotiable, this does not hold true for the full range of media vehicles. Newspaper space is rarely negotiable, but magazine space often is. The policy on rate negotiation is determined by the management of each individual magazine. Some print media will reduce editorial pages before cutting advertising costs. Others will negotiate off their rate card, and still others will stick to their rate cards but offer premium position (such as running your ad in the first few pages of the publication) at no extra charge.

When placing media directly, your first step will be to contact the broadcast and print vehicles and obtain standard rates and media kits from your assigned reps. Prior to any negotiation, examine all of your options. Then make sure your reps know you have a variety of alternative vehicles in which to spend your media dollars. Let them know that your dollars are precious and few, so you must get the best value for your media investment.

Certainly, agencies, media buying services, and even list brokers are better equipped to obtain the best buys and issue the proper paperwork. Standard industry practice requires buys to be executed by insertion or broadcast orders, and schedule revisions are made via change orders. Of course, no media should be placed by your agency or buying service until you have approved their proposed media schedule detailing insertion or air dates, ad sizes, frequency, and ad or schedule costs.

To help you obtain the best buys for your media dollars, it's helpful to understand some of the technical jargon used by the media and agencies. The following are a few definitions which will come in handy when buying space and time.

CIRCULATION.   The total number of copies sold or distributed.

REACH.   In print, reach is the percentage of a given market or percentage of the universe to which you are selling. In broadcast, reach is a percentage of a geographically-defined market. For example, your radio spot buy might reach 65 percent of women aged 25 to 49 in the area of dominant influence (ADI).

FREQUENCY.   The number of times an average audience (readers or listeners) is exposed to the message. This is not the total number of spots or ads. The frequency required depends on the complexity of the message, the advertising environment, and the effectiveness of the creative, among other factors. In trade publications, the average ad page is usually noted by 70 percent of the readership base.

UNIT COST.   The cost per ad or spot.

COST PER THOUSAND.   The cost to reach one thousand people through any medium. It's the basic unit by which direct mail lists are sold and a means of comparing efficiency. For example, you may compare the cost to reach one thousand readers of two competing publications.

COST PER POINT.   A means for measuring broadcast efficiency, the cost to reach 1 percent of the total ADI. Technically speaking, your agency will look at your total broadcast buy in terms of the total points necessary. Points are an expression of reach multiplied by frequency. For example, to reach 60 percent of the market three times equals 180 rating points.

RATINGS. A means for measuring broadcast audience, ratings are an expression of the total numbers of radio listeners or television viewers. Ratings vary by program and daypart and control how much you can expect to pay for your spot. Costs may also be higher for a daypart with lower ratings but which is in high demand by advertisers. And you can expect to pay more to reach fewer people if the audience is better qualified. For example, if your target audience is made up of physicians and a particular television show targets them specifically, then you can expect to pay a higher cost for your spot, even though the overall ratings or viewer numbers may be low.

AUDIT STATEMENTS. Publications are audited to guarantee to advertisers the publisher is reporting the actual number of readers. Audit statements provide in-depth information as to the readership itself, geographic and professional information, and what percentage of the readers pay for the publication.

AGENCY COMMISSIONS. Most media pay a standard 15 percent commission to recognized agencies and buying services. In effect, the agency is billed 15 percent less for commissionable media and marks up their own invoice to you, the client, thereby realizing, upon your payment, a 15 percent commission. Noncommissionable media (those which do not charge 15 percent less to recognized agencies or buying services) are marked up to yield 15 percent commission above the actual cost of the media. In this case you, not the media, are paying the agency commission.

LIST RENTAL. Assembled from directories and Yellow Pages listings, "compiled lists" are less expensive to rent than those of subscribers or proven buyers. The more qualified or specialized the list, the more you can expect to pay. List costs are increased incrementally through the addition of "selects" or additional qualifiers such as household income, home ownership, and type of residence. List houses also have a variety of setup fees and minimum charges which will add to the list rental cost.

Three Ways To Use Public Relations To Stand Out From the Crowd

Public relations opportunities often seem limited when you run a one-person, home-based operation. Yet the same tenets of PR apply for small, home-based businesses as they do in large corporations. The thrust of every public relations program is to gain "free" media exposure. What's free, of course, is the print space or air time—acquired after countless hours of concentrated efforts. For home-based business owners, the biggest investment in public relations is in time, your most costly commodity. To maximize your return on time invested in public relations activities, your PR effort must be thoroughly planned and selectively targeted.

The importance of public relations cannot be overlooked. With effective PR, you will extend your message into media which might be inaccessible or unaffordable to you through paid advertising. Unlike paid advertising, however, you will have little control over the content and delivery of your message and even less control over frequency or timing of PR coverage. On the plus side, editorial or news coverage will undoubtedly be considered more credible by your target audience than information they obtain directly from your ads.

Special Promotions Win Publicity

Home-based business owners are often successful in using limited funds to create promotions targeting the small number of writers, reporters, and editors who have direct influence over the media which reach their principal target audiences. Overloaded by a bombardment of press releases, photographs, press kits, invitations to conferences, and other standard PR approaches, writers and editors often respond favorably to promotions which focus their attention in a clever or unusual way on a unique product or service story of special interest to their audiences.

For example, when Ken D. began promoting special executive getaway packages for two as an incentive to corporate clients, he also launched a special promotion to key travel and local business press. Reporters and editors received "Make Your Own Getaway" kits. The kits contained all the components—in miniature—of a fantasy vacation on a remote beach. Two tiny lounge chairs, a beach umbrella, sunglasses, and two drinking cups were included in the boxed mailings. A one-page release was enclosed which focused on his company's unique new approach to rewarding corporate travelers.

Because Ken's idea was in fact unique, new, and in many cases bold, his fantasy getaway promotion to writers and editors successfully yielded national publicity in the important trade press as well as several local mentions. Reprints of the editorial coverage obtained in national trade publications were then used in sales literature targeting corporate accounts.

Unique mailings to writers and editors have also been a large part of the special promotions conducted by Ginnie and Sam P. to promote their exotic potted herbs. In conjunction with the launch of a new, small-space mail order advertising campaign to promote their gourmet selections, Ginnie and Sam sent samples to key press. The gourmet selection itself featured three exotic herb plants nestled in three-inch pots packaged in wooden crates filled with Spanish moss, with beautifully designed and printed labels completing the upscale look of the product.

For the press, Ginnie and Sam included a sheet of printed information focusing on the uniqueness of the product and its special appeal to the recipients' readers, their environmental, all-natural approach to growing, plus a succinct paragraph on their company's background. Also included was a color product release photo with an appropriate caption.

Ginnie and Sam's publicity efforts yielded several photo and editorial mentions in some of the country's most upscale home, garden, and gourmet magazines. The publicity virtually doubled or tripled the reach of their conservative, small-space advertising campaign, stimulated sales, and provided the income necessary to begin formulation of catalog materials.

Special Events That Get You Noticed

Participation in special events offers home-based business owners an opportunity to shine. Kathleen M.'s participation in a local showhouse for charity engendered extensive publicity for her interior design firm. Before she committed her services, Kathleen determined that the showhouse would be covered by a local magazine well read by her target audience and would also receive several mentions in the Home section of her city's metropolitan daily newspaper.

Participation in the showhouse was essentially guaranteed to help Kathleen gain publicity and stand out from the crowd. But not all types of events offer home-based business owners this type of singular publicity. When planning your own PR program, beware of any event in which your company's message might "get lost" or buried in the crowd of messages for the event itself or by other participants.

For example, after several months in business, Mike T.'s real estate firm was invited to participate in a local festival celebrating the twentieth anniversary of the community. Instead of providing a unique opportunity for his company to shine, Mike's tiny booth was nondescript and hardly visible among the hundreds of other booths lining the main thoroughfare. Those who came by his booth were happy to pick up the free buttons, balloons, and other giveaways, but Mike in turn had no way of knowing whether they were potential home buyers or sellers. Consequently, the event could not be directly traced to any appreciable new business.

Selecting a New Angle for Your Seminar

Seminars, as detailed in Chapter 5, offer you the opportunity to establish yourself as expert. If the content of your seminar is unique or contains information that is new or difficult to obtain elsewhere, your seminar content may be of interest to select press. Mark B. works hard to establish himself as an accounting and financial planning expert for small businesses by hosting seminars on "business survival during a recession," for small business owners. The content of his talk is summarized into "ten steps for surviving the recession," and distributed to the press along with a company backgrounder and release. Though not widely picked up by the press, several smaller publications have printed Mark's "ten steps." He in turn has reprinted their coverage and uses it as a promotional tool for additional seminars.

Playing It Straight: Traditional Ways of Making News

In the information age you might think, with the public's appetite for news, that making news would be easy. In truth, making news today is harder than ever without resorting to strange, bizarre, outlandish, or controversial angles. But there is still plenty of room for traditional public relations efforts and stories, provided they fill the specific needs of the targeted press. What do writers, editors, and reporters want?

They're looking for anything that is real news or of special interest to their readers, listeners, or viewers. In short, the needs of the press will vary depending on the needs of their own individual audiences. The problem for the press is that too much information is circulated to them which is not newsworthy or interesting.

When landscape architect Hunter C. received a national award for a unique naturalistic landscaping project, his award was of special interest to the Home and Garden editor of the local newspaper, who picked up information from the release and even called Hunter for further information and background for the story he prepared. The award itself was not news of special interest to the national horticultural publications, but the uniqueness of the garden design which prompted the award garnered significant coverage. To publicize the award, Hunter tailored his message to the specific needs of each type of press. Instead of sending out a uniform release, he tailored the story angles according to the reporters' special needs.

As Leisha's home-based business grew, stories about her company and its maternity products were of interest to different types of media. At first, her product was so novel that local newspapers and other general press wrote product and emerging business stories. With the growth of her product line, Leisha's company drew the attention of gift and specialty store trade press. Later, her company was labeled a dramatic success story by the national business press, which found her innovative corporate structure and personal philosophy of special interest.

Your first step in establishing a PR program will be to create a press list which contains the names of all media with editors or reporters who will find your company's product or service messages of special interest to their readers, viewers, or listeners. Depending upon the type of information your company disseminates, you may wish to include local newspapers, magazines, radio and television program producers, regional business publications, national trade publications, and possibly even national business publications. Any large public library will be a good source for public relations directories such as *Burrelle's*. Be certain the list you develop addresses individuals by name and not by title alone, such as "news editor."

For written press releases, use a standard format with a contact name and telephone number at the top. The headline centered below should summarize the pertinent news item, such as "Sally Jones Appointed President of Sales Strategy, Inc." Keep your release to one page with flush-left paragraphs. Begin your first paragraph with the city and date (you may choose to omit a date to eliminate time sensitivity).

The city and date are followed by your first paragraph, or hook. Remember, this is not a sales piece. For proper style, read several articles on page one of your daily newspaper and approximate the style and tone you find there. Present your facts succinctly and crisply. Use quotations which are fact-filled, informative, and compelling. Use the last paragraph to provide standard background information on your company and its products or services. All paragraphs should be no longer than a few sentences.

When disseminating single releases, it may be helpful to use your fax machine instead of the mail for distribution. This adds to the feeling of urgency and shortens the time span between dissemination and your follow-up phone call. Or consider sending releases, and even articles, on diskette so editors can easily work with them.

If you are introducing a unique product or service, and public relations is to become a large part of your ongoing marketing communications effort, a press kit should be developed which includes a company backgrounder or fact sheet and other explanatory, supporting, or informative materials. This is not a sales kit, however, and all materials must directly relate to the needs of the writers' or editors' audiences. Include 3-inch-by-5-inch or 5-inch-by-7-inch black-

and-white photographs, and always tape a typewritten caption to each.

Often, photos and captions are used to fill "holes" at publication time, and the suburban or neighborhood papers make excellent use of photo releases. To help the press utilize your submitted photography, be certain the photos are not the usual static shots, such as of one person handing an award to another. Use humor and an interesting approach. Photographs of people (particularly children) are most desirable.

Telephone contact with the press is vital to successful placement. It's unreasonable to expect to fax or mail releases, kits, or diskettes and obtain positive results without follow up. Prior to your call, prepare as you would for a cold call to a prospect. Ask yourself why your story or topic will be of special interest to that reporter's or editor's audience. Then be prepared to present that information in your opener. And be sensitive to the writer's or editor's deadlines and needs. Be prepared to turn around additional information immediately, or call back several times when the reporter has more time for a lengthy discussion.

Few home-based business owners would attempt to handle major press conferences without professional assistance. Should the need arise, consider employing a public relations or public affairs firm which will handle your conference on an *ad hoc* or project basis, including all the necessary telephone follow-up, releases, or article placements.

Another means for positioning yourself or your company as expert is to write articles for publication. You may choose to create a short article or piece and distribute it to a variety of publications. Or work directly with an editor of a trade publication, for example, to supply a technical article which meets the publication's specific requirements. If your background includes training or experience in writing, then this public relations tactic is tailor-made for you. Smaller publications, such as weekly newspapers, often rely on editorials submitted by non-staff writers, and some use local experts to write weekly columns. Generally there is little or no compensation involved. But these are plum opportunities which can position you as an expert in your given field and may become an ongoing source of lead generation.

Alex S., the public relations practitioner mentioned in previous chapters, writes articles for trade publications that target his best prospects. This is essential to building his company image and raising awareness of his firm among key target audiences.

In all, target your public relations campaign as you might any advertising or other marketing communications program. Plan carefully to engage in only those activities you can support year-round and those which enable you and your firm to stand out from the crowd, cut through the clutter, and communicate directly with your best prospects through media which lend credibility to your message. If you plan an extensive public relations campaign, consider hiring a public relations agency. Most work on a fee or retainer basis and handle press contact, releases, press kits and back-grounders, and clipping services. They often have good working relationships with the media which have taken years to develop.

Armed with the fundamentals of media planning and placement, you now have the tools to formulate budgets and plans that generate leads and support sales growth. Use of the media will help you build your business on a scale virtually unattainable through direct sales alone. As a home-based business owner you may have a limited budget, but through careful and selective use of the media you can narrowly target your audiences to reach just the prospects you need to help your business grow.

chapter eight

Six Steps to Keeping Lead Generation on Track

By now you've seen how programs for sales and marketing communications are inextricably bound together. For home-based business owners, all programs must work in unison to drive company growth. Marketing communications must work hard to support sales by supplying qualified leads or effectively moving prospects along in the sales cycle. Too many costly errors, such as changes in marketing communications direction, sporadic efforts, or lack of focus, can have dramatic repercussions, not the least of which is a fall-off in sales. These and other expensive mistakes happen primarily because of a failure to plan for marketing communications.

Just as it's critical to maintain a consistent, proactive sales program to keep sales on an even keel, a written marketing communications plan keeps activities and budgets on track year-round. In the previous chapters, you have acquired all the pieces of the marketing communications puzzle.

- You know how to present your product or service so it is most appealing to prospects.
- You have identified and profiled your target prospects.

- You have created a marketing communications plat-form as a foundation for all communications mes-sages.
- You have prepared a list of the tools and materials necessary to work with cold, warm, and hot prospects.
- You understand basic media principles and can focus on those media which best reach your target audiences.
- You have a relative idea of costs and annual budgets.

Now, just pull all the pieces of the puzzle together for a look at the big picture. It's just a matter of "quick assembly" into a comprehensive, year-long plan which is both economical and effective in generating leads and supporting sales growth.

If you plan to use an agency or design firm, you may be asking yourself, Why do I need to do this? Won't my vendor do this for me? Indeed, your agency or design firm may do some planning for you. They may handle media planning and actual execution of the tools and materials. But the homework which must be accomplished beforehand deter-mines in many cases the success or failure of what will be developed by your agency or design group.

Your Marketing Communications Blueprint ─────────

Just as a business plan keeps your company on track, a good marketing communications plan is a blueprint for action that will perform a number of highly critical functions. A market-ing communications plan can:

- help you save money by avoiding any unnecessary or impulsive expenditures;
- enable you to focus on long-range strategies;
- permit coordination of communications activities with the ongoing management of your firm;

- help you to integrate all aspects of marketing communications;
- prevent important communications activities from falling by the wayside during even the busiest times of the year.

Each day and from every direction, you are bombarded by a multitude of marketing communications opportunities and choices such as the following.

- You are asked to participate in a local business fair.
- A radio station approaches you for a "special" run of station (ROS) advertising package.
- A new directory is being published and solicits your advertising.
- A direct mail company pitches you on "marriage mail," an insert which is packaged and delivered with those of other advertisers.
- A national trade publication pitches you on advertising in an "off" month when there will be a special editorial focus.
- A video production company calls and wants to shoot a video news release (VNR) on your company's business services and place it on local news shows around the country.

Sound familiar? With a written marketing communications plan in hand, you can easily evaluate each opportunity or media offer to determine whether it targets the right prospects, is consistent with your marketing communications goals, fits within the established budget, and whether it will be as good for your business or better than other planned activities.

The following examples show how a written marketing communications plan becomes a yardstick for measuring the feasibility of new or additional choices.

1. When asked to participate in a local business fair, you evaluate the opportunity by comparing those prospects you are likely to meet there with the profile of your primary target audience. Then examine the budget section of your plan to see whether the cost of participating in the fair will mean replacement of other activities which more directly generate new business.

2. To evaluate the radio station's ROS (run of station) offer, you review the media section of your plan to determine whether the time of day spots run is important to penetration of your target prospect groups. If, for example, you can best reach your audience in afternoon drive time, then a schedule of ROS spots which can run any time of the day or night is not an effective buy for you.

3. New directories are being published all the time and are continually soliciting your advertising. If your media strategy includes a focus on search corridor advertising, use of an additional directory might be a good idea provided its readers match your target audience profile and the directory will be published in sufficient quantity to penetrate that audience while supplying useful information to them.

4. Marriage mail is often used by advertisers who wish to make a special price or coupon offer to all households within a given geographic market area. When pitched on using marriage mail, a quick review of your marketing communications platform will let you know whether this type of advertising will cheapen your image or, conversely, provide a strong incentive to prospects to take advantage of a special pricing offer.

5. If your current media schedule calls for national advertising in trade publications, you will be frequently pitched by their reps on adding insertions in months for which your advertising is not scheduled. One inducement they may offer is a special article or editorial focus which will be of interest to your target audience. To evaluate these offers, you will simply review the media strategy section of your plan. If certain months are identified there as "off" months when your target audience is less likely to be reading trade publications, no matter the editorial focus, adding an insertion will not meet your marketing communications needs. On the other hand, if the special editorial feature is to appear during a period of high readership, then you may consider moving an insertion scheduled for another issue or increasing your budget by adding an insertion.

6. Video news releases (VNRs) are becoming increasingly popular. If you offer a consumer product or service to a wide geographic market area, the opportunity to have a VNR created and placed may be consistent with your company's goals, reach your target audiences, and fall within the confines of your marketing communications budget. But if you offer a business service or products, placement of a VNR on consumer news shows may represent a significant drain on your established budget to reach a large broadcast audience of individuals who do not meet your target audience profile.

As you can see, your written marketing communications plan will keep you focused on the big picture and help you to avoid costly mistakes.

The following six-step plan uses the same format for creating hard-working marketing communications plans as that implemented by major U.S. corporations.

Assemble Your Own Marketing Communications Plan

Just follow this simple outline to develop your own annual marketing communications plan. It need not be lengthy or complicated—a brief outline or series of bulleted items may work best for you.

1. Situation analysis
- Challenges
- Position in the marketplace

- Competition
- Other factors

2. **Target audience**
   - Profile of primary audience
   - Secondary audience

3. **Objectives**
   - List of goals for marketing communications

4. **Strategies**
   - Marketing communications platform
   - Marketing tools
   - Advertising
   - Public relations
   - Special promotions
   - Direct mail
   - Research
   - Media rationale
   - Media schedule

5. **Tactics**
   - Dates for specific activities

6. **Budget**
   - Production
   - Printing
   - Media
   - Miscellaneous

Step 1. Prepare a Situation Analysis

Your first step is to take a comprehensive look at your company's challenges, its position in the marketplace, its competition, and any other factors which will affect your strategies for marketing communications. Like your company's business plan, this is an internal working document, so you can be honest and direct when describing the ways your company's strengths or weaknesses will influence the way you communicate and the content of your company's messages. Elements such as pricing, company size and age, location, uniqueness of your product or service, undercapitalization, the impact of direct and perceived competition, and any other pertinent elements should be addressed in the situation analysis. A year from now, when updating your marketing communications plan, you may be surprised by the extent to which your situation will have changed. Your overall plan can then be easily adapted to correspond with those changes.

Ken D.'s executive travel service, introduced in Chapter 7, has experienced dramatic growth in its first two years of operation. Much of that growth can be directly attributed to judicious use of radio advertising, public relations, and special promotions. Housed in what was an in-law apartment over his two-car garage, Ken's company employs three commissioned travel agents/planners and an office manager.

A separate telephone service bureau handles incoming leads generated by radio advertising, which come in from three cities on a toll-free telephone number. Customer service operators input the lead information into Ken's software database, and leads are sent by modem each night to his office manager for distribution to the three in-house agents.

All information is manipulated on-screen, and the agents are set up with networked terminals. When not working leads, they are expected to cold call from a list of businesses rented exclusively for telemarketing purposes. Ken's job is to work directly with larger corporate prospects and clients to help them plan for the most advantageous use of their company travel dollars.

Although Ken uses an agency to produce sales and marketing communications tools and to plan and place media, each year he updates his own marketing communications plan and incorporates the agency-supplied media schedules and budgets into his own document. An excerpt drawn from the situation analysis he is preparing for his company's third year in operation might look like this:

> After a period of exponential growth, the company's focus in the coming fiscal year will be to stabilize growth and focus on increasing profitability. In the past year, a large volume of new accounts have been generated which are not uniformly productive or profit intensive. Marketing communications activities must be adapted to target larger, high-volume accounts and support a sales effort which directly targets major businesses which have not previously responded to our advertising.
>
> Radio advertising in the three target markets will be cut back during those weeks or months which have proven to be less productive. Radio advertising in Boston, our most expensive market, should be scaled back while we attempt to recontact all leads generated from our advertising in that city which have not converted to sales.
>
> Overcoming stiff competition remains our most significant challenge. Prospects who have established relationships with travel agencies or consultants are hesitant to change, particularly when they are based out of town. Until now, outside of our Make Your Own Getaway incentive, we have had little to offer those prospects as a major incentive to switch to our company. So this year we will launch a new level of service with designated agents on call 24 hours a day to handle travel scheduling emergencies. In addition, we will launch a new pricing arrangement which features discounted rates (or reduced commissions) on all accounts. This will mandate an immediate change in our marketing communications focus which, when properly packaged, should provide the necessary incentive for our prospects who are happy with their present travel services or consultants to make the switch to our firm.

Christine N. is a talented glass artist whose blown vases, perfume bottles, and paperweights recall the elegant curved shapes and decorative designs reminiscent of the art nouveau era. Thanks to resurging interest in glass from that period and Chris's fine work, the items sell well both at regional and national shows and in a handful of jewelry and gift stores. Chris carries an extremely full load, handling sales, marketing communications, product design and production, and even order processing and shipping in-house—all with the help of a single glass artisan and a part-time shipping and order-processing clerk. But Chris plans major changes in the management of her company and is revising her marketing communications plan accordingly.

Customer acceptance of the price increases has been favorable. Sales of products in the $60 to $85 range remain strong, and store owners report satisfactory sales of items marked up to $120. Show sales continue to be the principal income generator, although the incidence of large orders from stores should continue to increase and could potentially become the principal income generator for the company. To pursue jewelry and gift store orders, a rep company will be contracted with to sell all products on a commission basis to chains and specialty stores nationwide. This will free me from sales tasks and return me to the studio to supervise production and create new designs.

As orders increase, management of public relations, direct mail, and small-space advertising should be entrusted to a local ad agency. This firm will also be required to produce catalogues, order forms, and any additional sales tools needed by the new reps.

Step 2: Identify the Target Audiences

Following a short one- or two-page situation analysis, briefly summarize the characteristics of your target audience. If you have more than one target group, list them as primary, secondary, and so on. The bulk of your marketing communications efforts and expenditures will then be directed to reaching and penetrating your primary audience with smaller budgets and fewer activities directed toward secondary or tertiary groups. If your target audiences are to be treated or addressed equally, this should be made clear in your target audience profile.

The target audience for Ken's executive travel service is somewhat difficult to narrowly define. Essentially, it may be anyone who participates in corporate travel decision making. The titles can include corporate travel planner, sales manager, and secretary. Ken primarily relies on radio advertising, and his target audience is loosely defined as adults aged 25 to 54.

This simple target audience profile, "adults aged 25 to 54 who participate in corporate travel decision making," is actually specific enough for his agency to make educated marketing communications buys and recommendations. By accessing audience research information (such as through Scarborough or MRI), the agency is able to determine those radio stations with the highest number of listeners in the target age group who also fit the travel decision making criteria. Based on Ken's basic target audience profile, his agency can also select and place small-space ads in those trade publications which are read by the largest number of corporate travel decision makers as well as rent their subscriber lists for telemarketing purposes.

So you see, your target audience profile, no matter how simple, is integral to all marketing communications strategies and execution.

Step 3: State Your Objectives

Your next task is to outline your marketing communications objectives. Consider your long-term goals and state each objective in concise, short sentences. It may even help to bullet them. They should be easily understood and, in some cases, measurable. If you use an agency, for example, it will be easier for them to know when they have met your expectations if one of your goals is to "increase leads from advertising by 10 percent." But remember, everyone is frustrated by unachievable goals—even you. So the goals you cite in your marketing communications plan must be realistic and achievable.

Here is an example of the types of marketing communications objectives set by Christine's glass studio.

- Reduce show participation to only eight shows per year.

- Create sales tools for new reps, including catalogue reprints and order forms.

- Interview and contract with a marketing communications agency to produce and place advertising, direct mail and public relations.

- Increase the frequency of direct mail to retail prospects to three times per year.

- Revise the small-space trade advertising campaign to feature more upscale products.

- Place at least one photograph and product mention of a vase or paperweight in one of the targeted home publications such as HG.

Step 4: Formulate Strategies for Creative Production and Media Placement

The strategies section is the core of your marketing communications plan. It contains a complete breakdown of the activities you believe are required to achieve your objectives. Start by inserting your marketing communications platform as page one of this section. Then describe the marketing tools whose creative content will be based on the messages contained in your marketing communications platform. State the purpose of each tool. Describe how and why advertising, public relations, and special promotions are to be used; when direct mail is to be utilized and who will receive it; and whether market research is indicated.

Following the description of your strategies for what will be produced and why, detail your strategies for media usage— how your messages will reach the target audiences. Your media rationale may be as simple as a list of publications (where ads will appear), ad sizes, and costs followed by a media schedule showing insertion dates (when). More complex media rationales and schedules, such as those supplied by agencies, may include a full description of each media vehicle and the rationale behind its selection, plus charts and graphs which plot the schedule on a weekly or monthly basis.

Before Regina hired a creative copy and design team to execute the marketing communications and other materials for her events and conference planning company, she outlined a marketing communications strategy. It contained a brief description of the tools and programs she deemed essential to position her company against powerful competition. The company identity package would include a logo treatment, letterhead and envelopes, and business and Rolodex cards. For sales support, she required a company brochure or folder with inserts, an appropriate-sized envelope and adhesive mailing labels, a foldover card with a blank interior and matching envelope to be used for personal follow-up with prospects, and a cover or binder to customize large proposals. Marketing communications tools for her business-to-business campaign would include small-space advertising and affordable direct mail. Beyond this, few specifics were outlined in the strategies section of her marketing communications plan—that is, until she engaged the services of her team.

At this juncture, it was decided that the basic package of company materials would be printed in two colors, teal and gray, on white stock to enhance color brightness. All paper stocks, with the exception of the 25 percent cotton letterhead and matching envelopes, would be coated to minimize ink absorption or bleeding. After much discussion, it was concluded that the company brochure would be created as a four-color, four-panel folder with a die-cut rear pocket and full-length tab reading "Events and Conference Planning." This format was selected to accommodate four-color photography which would be used to "demonstrate" the company's capabilities in all types of events, conference planning and execution. The rear pocket would be die-cut to carry a business card but not glued, and the black-and-white inserts would all be 8½-inches-by-11-inches, not graduated in height, to shave the hefty cost of gluing and die-cutting inserts from the printing bill.

The inserts themselves would vary depending upon how the brochure/folder was being used. When mailed as a follow-up to a qualified prospect, the inserts would include a sales letter on letterhead and up to three case histories or examples demonstrating Regina's company's range of services. These one-color case histories would be printed on matching coated stock and include photography, layout, and copy which would also be reproduced in a corresponding campaign of three black-and-white, small-space ads. By relying on the same original artwork to produce both the ads and inserts, Regina's company would reinforce the key selling points made in the advertising campaign while extending its reach to key prospects—and reduce her production cost significantly.

Cover art for the folder would also serve double duty. A slight modification, consisting of a one-color overlay to include the company address, would become matching artwork for proposal covers. The covers would be printed on one side only along with the four-panel folder. In this way, Regina would save significant sums on both production and printing of proposal covers. This would also give her a flexible proposal tool to be used either as the cover of a spiral-bound proposal or to customize the cover of a standard three-ring binder—the kind with a transparent cover sleeve.

In addition to the three case histories, an additional sales support tool would be produced as an insert to the folder for use in first meetings with prospects. A two-color "event planner worksheet" would be a handy tool for taking new prospects through the process of planning a hypothetical event in order to demonstrate the ways Regina and her company would expertly manage every detail. Short letter proposals would simply take the place of the standard inserts in the rear of the company folder when used as part of a sales presentation.

Direct mail production would also be affordable, yet tie in to the key selling points and themes of the advertising and folder inserts. Two, 6-inch-by-9-inch two-color direct mail pieces would be designed with matching envelopes. The large size would help the envelope gain attention, and the envelope itself would increase the mailer's chances of getting past screeners.

Once Regina had developed these concepts with the help of her creative team, she went back and modified the strategies section of her marketing communications plan to include a page or two summarizing them. In this way, as all tools and programs were developed, she was able to keep the production focused and on track—and in accordance with the original strategies which had been carefully and deliberately developed.

Christine N. plans less elaborate marketing communications strategies to build sales of her glass vases, perfume bottles, and paperweights. Here is a short excerpt from the strategies section of her marketing communications plan.

> Direct mail will be used to target jewelry and gift store owners. Mailings will take place July, September, and November. Each mailing will include three components, a four-color, 6-inch-by-9-inch postcard with a short sales message, and wholesale prices of the items pictured on the back. Each of the three photographs will depict a cross-section of products from each product line. They will be mailed inside

6-inch-by-9-inch envelopes with a cover letter on matching stationery. The letter will describe the products and how well they are received by customers of jewelry and gift store owners nationwide. The July letter will emphasize stocking products for Christmas sales, the September mailing will be geared toward Valentine's Day sales, and the November mailing will emphasize springtime wedding gifts.

The list itself will be drawn from the subscriber list of XYZ Magazine. Each mailing will be in a quantity of 5,000, with the first 2,500 established as a control group to receive each of the three mailings. The second group of 2,500 names will receive the second mailing along with the control group, as will the third group of 2,500 subscribers to receive the third mailing. In the first quarter, the results of the direct mail prospecting campaign will be reviewed to determine if the three-time frequency to the control group was more successful than the single mailings to the remainder of the list.

Also in July, September, and November, our current retail customers will receive the postcards alone, without the cover letter or envelope, as a reminder to order early for the gift-giving seasons. Based on the results of these postcard mailings to current customers, we may produce additional postcards for mailings in February and the following spring.

The content of our one-third page, four-color trade ads will be revised. More upscale products, such as our newest large vases, will be pictured, and we will continue to offer our four-color catalogs free.

For public relations purposes, the same three photographs shot for the postcards will be mailed to key editors and reporters on our PR list. The four-color photographs will be captioned with product descriptions and accompanied by releases which focus on the resurgence in popularity of art nouveau style glass.

Chris's media rationale and short schedule are also easy to summarize and prepare. As she primarily reaches her consumer buyers through direct selling at craft shows or through public relations, Chris's advertising focuses on use of just two trade publications targeting jewelry and gift store owners. With help from the magazines' sales reps, she has selected a schedule based on the most favorable months in which to reach her target audience through these publications. She has also obtained merchandising perks, such as product photos and editorial mentions, due to participation in select issues.

Chris's schedule simply lists the months in which her ads will appear followed by ad sizes and costs. She also lists the months in which her product mentions will appear in order to simplify lead tracking.

The media rationale and schedules for Ken's executive travel service are much more complex. His print advertising includes various directory ads, small-space black-and-white trade publication ads targeting corporate travel planners, and ads in special travel planning issues of select business newspapers and magazines in three cities. A separate radio schedule is also required for his complex three-market buy.

Fortunately, his agency provides comprehensive, easy-to-read print and broadcast schedules following a short media rationale. Ken adds these agency-supplied pages to the strategy section of his marketing communications plan. His office manager also keeps copies of the schedules on her desk in order to help her identify and track how the numbers of incoming leads (which she receives by modem from the service bureau) rise and fall in relation to the radio spot schedules.

Sample Print and Broadcast Schedules

To help you prepare your own print advertising schedule, here is a sample format which you may adapt for your own use. If you are placing your own artwork with the publications, it will be helpful to include materials' closing dates on your schedule. These dates are well in advance of publication and may be found in the media kits provided to you by the publications.

Media Advertising January - June

publication	freq of pub	circl % pd	freq rate	Jan	Feb	Mar	Apr	May	Jun	# of ads	total	gross imps*
ABC Magazine	22	130,398 100.0%	6X		2/12 1/3 Pg 4/c $3,650 (Close 12/18)	3/12 1/3 Pg 4/c $3,650 (Close 1/15)		5/12 1/3 Pg 4/c $3,650 (Close 1/15)		3	$10,950	391,194
DEF Magazine	52	168,210 5.7%	3X	1/14 & 21 Showcase $1,900 (Close 12/19)	2/11 Showcase $950 (Close 1/16)		4/15 Showcase $950 (Close 3/14)			4	$3,800	672,840
GHI Magazine	12	159,002 0.0%	1X			3/1 1/3 Pg 4/c $3,300 (Close 2/4)				1	$3,300	159,002
Totals:				$1,900	$4,600	$6,950	$950	$3,650	$0	8	$18,050	1,054,826

Avg CMP:** $17.11
Total: $18,050

* gross impressions = total readers
** CPM = cost per thousand

While it's unlikely you will prepare your own broadcast schedules, you may have to evaluate or work with those provided by an agency or media buying service. The following example shows an effective radio schedule format. It's easy to read and contains all necessary information including an overview, a breakdown of the buy and costs per station, and a flowchart showing the schedule in broadcast weeks.

Schedule Synopsis

Stations:

- WAA-FM
- WBBB-FM
- WCCC-FM

Schedule duration:

- Seven weeks of advertising per station, in two flights.
- The first flight begins the week of September 23; the second begins the week of November 4.
- Start dates with each station will be staggered to maximize length of coverage.

Target audience: Women 25–44

Schedule reach: 25.4 percent

Schedule frequency: 17.5

Target Rating Points: 444.0

Cost Per Point (unadjusted): 55.00

Total Cost: $24,430

Cost Per Point (Unadjusted): $55.00
Total Cost: $24,430

station	daypart	number of spots	program	spot cost	weekly total	7 week total
WAAA-FM	M-F 6A-10A	4	News/Traffic	$150	$600	
	M-F 10A-3P		Sponsorship			
		4	Mid-day	85	340	
	M-F 3P-7P	3	Afternoon Drive	110	330	
					$1,270	$8,890
WBBB-FM	M-F 6A-9A	4	Morning Drive	125	500	
	M-F 10A-3P	5	Mid-day	80	400	
	M-F 3P-7P	3	Afternoon Drive	100	300	
	M-F 8P-12M	5	Evening	20	100	
	SU 7P-9P	2	Special			
			Programming	40	80	
					$1,380	$9,660
WCCC-FM	M-F 6A-8A	4	Morning Drive	75	300	
	M-F 10A-3P	4	Mid-day	45	180	
	M-F 3P-7P	3	Afternoon Drive	45	135	
	M-F 7P-10P	5	Special			
			Programming	45	225	
	M-S 6A-3P	5	Daytime			
			Rotation	N/C	N/C	
					$ 840	$5,880

Schedule Total: $24,430

	Week of:									
station	**23**	**30**	**07**	**14**	**21**	**28**	**04**	**11**	**18**	**25**	**02**
WAAA-FM	■	■	■	■			■	■	H	■
WBBB-FM		■	■	■	■		■	■	O L I	■
WCCC-FM		■	■	■	■	■	■	■	D A Y	
Broadcast Month	Sept.	October				November				December	

Step 5: Plot Your Tactics

With the bulk of your planning complete, simply set up an annual calendar which delineates your tactics. Review each section of your strategies and assign dates for specific activities. This should be in the form of a monthly breakdown and look very much like a simple flow chart. You might also want to plot your tactics on your personal calendar, especially if you're not in the habit of referring to your marketing communications plan on a regular basis. Or consider plotting your schedule of activities on the software you use for sales tracking so you will be notified of pending marketing communications activities just as you are for sales call follow-up. But no matter how you track the activities, they must be scheduled to coordinate, without interference, with the day-to-day management of your growing business.

Interior designer Kathleen M. is always careful not to schedule advertising during the period in which she will be participating in an annual showhouse for charity. She is particularly careful to avoid scheduling prospecting activities, which include visiting new homeowners to drop off promotional materials, during the two weeks before the showhouse opening.

Ken never schedules out-of-town visits with clients during the second week of a new radio advertising campaign. He knows, by that time, that leads will have built to a level which will require him to spend long days and evenings in the office assisting his three agents in follow-up activities.

If you begin setting up schedules for execution of marketing communications tactics only to find you'll have too much to do in too little time, rethink your strategies. There may indeed be thousands of ways to grow your business, but you will only have time and energy to follow through on a limited few. So scale back your strategies until the tactics, when plotted on your calendar, appear reasonable along with the day-to-day operation of your business. It's best to scale back now rather than try to execute too many strategies. That's when critical lead generating activities fall by the wayside, sending marketing communications plans—and the sales programs which rely on them—dangerously off track.

Step 6: Finalize a Budget

The final section of your marketing communications plan covers budget, and you'll want to be certain you have budget lines for production, printing, media, and any miscellaneous items which will come out of your marketing communications funds. Actual expenditures should be checked quarterly against your projected budget. Once planning has been done in this way, it's very easy to see which areas are going under or over budget.

The following example shows how to break out a first year marketing communications budget. If you draft your own projected budget and the total is unrealistically high, it's best to revise your strategies and tactics. Include fewer types of tools and materials. And use your existing budget to produce the highest quality materials possible. Your final total will establish a fixed annual marketing communications budget for your growing firm.

I. Production

Logo design and stationery package:
business cards, letterhead, envelopes,
Rolodex cards, mailing labels $1,200

Company brochure and matching cover
sheet, both two-color .1,400

Photography for two black-and-white
ads, company brochure, and sales

presentation (slides) including film
and processing (no models) 2,550–3,300

Advertising and direct mail: two half-page
black-and-white ads; a second version of each
with copy and art expanded to 8½ " x 11"
for direct mail 1,800

Veloxes: four sets (two per ad) $80

II. Printing

Letterhead and envelopes: 2,000 each, two-color
Rolodex and business cards: 500 each, two-color
Mailing labels: 1,000 each, two-color 950–1,150

Company brochure and cover sheets: 1,000
each, two-color. Brochure is 11" x 17" folding
to 8½ " x 11". Cover sheet is 8½" x 11" 1,850–2,100

Direct mail: 500 each of two 8½" x 11"
black-and-white pieces with photos 150

Cover letters: 500 each of two surprinted in
black on existing letterhead 40

III. Media

Print schedule total .4,730

IV. Miscellaneous

Postage; blank 9" x 12" envelopes; holiday
cards, thank you notes, etc. 750

Projected annual budget . . . . <u>$15,500–$16,700</u>

Use your long-range marketing communications plan
to continually measure, focus, and correct marketing communications progress as necessary. It's amazing how your
campaigns and strategies may begin to deviate six months
down the road. This is particularly true if you are dealing

with a large number of outside vendors, such as for design and production, advertising, direct marketing, and printing. But if all new proposals or ideas are reviewed in terms of how they conform to your goals, strategies, and long-range budgets, you'll save money and eliminate unnecessary expenditures.

chapter nine

Staying the Course: Do's and Don'ts for Successful Growth

Throughout this book, you have seen examples of how home-based business owners have adapted sales and marketing communications strategies to fit their own requirements and unique visions of what their companies should become. Some view their home offices as a starting place they hope to outgrow. Others prefer their companies to remain home-based, growing in sales volume and profitability though not necessarily in their number of personnel.

It's inevitable that Leisha E.'s maternity products company will soon move entirely out of her home office. In the long term, having the manufacturing facility and customer service in separate locations will provide a strong enough barrier to internal communications to require integration of all processes at one location. And Leisha's home office will once again become a place for evening and weekend work only.

Ken D., too, will move his executive travel service business out of the in-law suite over his garage. Right now it's bursting at the seams with three agents, an office manager, and himself in residence. In order to satisfy the vision Ken has of his growing company, he will simply be forced to seek larger quarters, perhaps with offices in three or more cities.

But it's not surprising that the bulk of today's home based business owners are right where they want to stay. For them, maintaining a steady flow of new business, generating increased income, and growing increasingly profitable are the keys to home-based business success.

Daryl R. can grow his PC maintenance business without necessitating a move from his home-based office, thanks to the structure of his firm. Daryl contracts with independent technicians, themselves home-based, who are in constant contact by telephone or with the help of beepers, often 24 hours a day. Several of the technicians are equipped with modems and send service reports directly to Daryl's home office.

As his company grows, Daryl will continue to contract with independent technicians. Now, all technicians meet in his office for a weekly group meeting. But as the company expands, Daryl will change its structure to accommodate growth. There will be teams of three technicians, each under the guidance of a team leader, and Daryl will meet with team leaders only on a regular basis.

Landscape architect Hunter C. is not concerned about adding additional associates or partners to his firm. Instead, he plans to increase profitability with the same number of personnel as his company builds a prominent reputation in its areas of unique specialization.

Like Hunter, Judy K. sees no need to move her jewelry design and manufacturing business from her home studio. Instead, she will increase the number of assistants from one to two full-time and, as necessary, utilize the services of outside companies for sales, order tracking, and marketing communications. She also expects to increase the price of her beautifully crafted products as they gain in popularity and demand for them increases.

To Susan B., growth means adding more large accounts for her wholesale distribution business. To accommodate or service those customers, she'll contract with additional "associates" or independent reps. As Susan and her associates are on the road visiting clients the majority of the time, only a limited in-house support staff will be required to work in her home office five days a week.

Each of these individuals is following the "rules" for growing their home-based businesses. Yet they are adapting them to fit their own personal goals and ideals.

Misconceptions To Avoid When Growing a Business

But not all home-based business owners can or will succeed. An astonishingly high percentage may limit their chances for success due to some common misconceptions concerning sales and marketing communications. What follows is a series of dangerous false beliefs—and the truths that will save you from them.

1. **False: A great product/service will sell itself.**

    True: Countless terrific products, services, and companies have vanished into oblivion by holding on to this most ancient misconception. The greatest product or service in the world can't sell if no one knows about it, understands why they should want or need it, can or will pay for it, or knows how to acquire it. There is simply no getting away from use of standard sales and marketing communications methods. Once established, a terrific product or service may indeed sell faster or in higher volume due to favorable word of mouth, but this can rarely be relied on to expand or grow a new business to any great degree.

2. **False: They have my literature, they'll call when they're ready to buy.**

    True: Never assume, because you have contacted them once and perhaps supplied literature, that prospects will remember or call on you when they are prepared to make a buying decision. If you're not asking repeatedly for the business and your competition is, chances are they'll win the business and you won't. For most home-based business owners and the majority of businesses today, frequent sales contact is vital to closing sales. Ongoing contact with prospects and, in many cases, customers, takes the form of follow-up calls, mailings and, often, on-site visits. In many industries, it takes months or even years to win new accounts. One thing is certain. Persistence pays off, particularly in generating new business.

3. **False: Advertising doesn't work.**

   True: Of course advertising works. American companies alone spend billions of hard-earned dollars on campaigns each year to sell virtually every type of product or service under the sun. In fact, so much is known about why and how advertising works there should be no question as to its efficacy for business. But the problem is there are so many variables—so many things that can go wrong in less-than-expert hands and under less-than-ideal conditions—that advertising often gets a bad rap. For example, when an ad doesn't work, is it the fault of creative development? Is the ad running in the right media? Is there enough frequency to penetrate the target audience? Is the message or offer wrong? Is the product or service itself the problem?

   With so much at stake, advertising strategies, development, and placement should be handled by experienced specialists. Advertising looks easy, but it's not. And when it doesn't work as it should, it can be difficult to determine what went wrong.

4. **False: I'll save money by creating my own ads and mailers. The less I spend on brochures, mailers, and other materials, the more money I can bank.**

True: Do-it-yourself efforts generally yield marginal results which will cost money in lost revenues in the long run. Short-term savings seldom yield long-term growth. Produce and print only quality materials to create an effective, high-quality image for your growing business.

5. **False: People in my field don't solicit business clients by phone.**

True: Belief in this myth can have devastating results. It's often perpetuated by individuals who have left mid-level or upper management positions in prominent corporations where they were not largely responsible for generating sales or leads. In truth, while there are some industries in which direct solicitation is still taboo, in the vast majority of cases cold or warm calling is at the heart of building long-term, business-to-business sales.

Even consultants who require only a handful of clients at any one time must use the telephone as a part of the new business process. In this instance, generally a mutual interest, friend, or associate is used as the hook or premise upon which the call is based. But without using the telephone, these individuals would be reduced to relying on "chance" meetings at business functions, meetings arranged by third parties, or introductory sales letters (only marginally effective) in order to get to know their top prospects. Unfortunately, few businesses can be built by such nonaggressive means.

6. **False: I never get business from cold or warm calling, so it's best to rely on referrals.**

True: Often, individuals who are less experienced in cold or warm calling expect unrealistically fast results. To build business over time, a combination of referrals and cold and warm calling will be required. Referrals generally yield quick results, as they have already expressed an interest in buying what you have to sell.

Warm calls, most often follow-up calls to leads generated by marketing communications, may take longer to close than referrals, depending on your type of business and whether they are responding to request more information or to purchase your product or service. Cold calls, by and large, lay the groundwork for future sales. They are the first step in educating your business prospect, qualifying him, and creating a need for your product or service.

Many times, however, impatience or faulty expectations are not at the crux of a businessperson's failure to be successful on the telephone. Attitude and skill play essential roles. Those who get poor results from telephone contact with prospects, even when timely, ongoing follow up is undertaken, should consider polishing their skills in consultative selling—uncovering and filling prospect needs in a friendly, noncombative way.

7. False: No one understands my business/product/service/company as I do, so I have to do just about everything myself.

True: This type of martyrdom may make someone look like a hero in a large corporation, but it can be the death of a small home-based business. Without delegating, subcontracting, or in some way sharing the load, company growth is limited to the level of work one person can effectively perform. For most of us, our time is better spent doing what we do best and delegating some tasks to in-house support or outside services. Also, one person's level of competence cannot be equal in all areas. Outside "experts" are a valuable resource for all businesses.

8. False: I don't expect much from prospect meetings. Most are just a waste of time.

True: Those who are unsuccessful in personal selling may simply reduce the number of prospect meetings—

and the opportunity to close sales—rather than look to the cause of the problem. Lack of success in prospect meetings can be attributed to meeting with less than qualified prospects, poor personal selling skills, failure to differentiate between what is being sold and what the customer wishes to buy, inadequate tools and materials, or even a failing in the product or service itself. Prospect meetings are too important and costly to allow any one factor to detract from their effectiveness.

9. **False: Presentations should be spontaneous. Besides, there's no time to rehearse.**

True: Someone with this attitude may get lucky and succeed on rare occasions. But by and large, the result will be bored, alienated, or angry audiences and lost opportunities for growth. When it comes to winning presentations, rehearsal pays off.

10. **False: If I send out lots of releases, something's bound to get picked up.**

True: Editors and reporters are interested in newsworthy items or those of special interest to their own audiences. A flood of paper from a single source may only cause the recipients to tune out future items which may indeed be newsworthy or of unique interest.

11. **False: I'll produce a quick, inexpensive brochure now and replace it when business picks up.**

True: As weeks turn to months and the quick-and-dirty brochure becomes the standard company marketing piece for the long haul, this may have significant repercussions. First, it can create a poor or low-quality impression for a business and its products or services. Second, additional, better-quality tools may be produced over time which do not coordinate with the original piece, resulting in lack of a cohesive image and an ineffective sales presentation. Third, it costs more in the long run to produce two different brochures to serve the same task. It's always best to produce quality materials which work together as a unit to make a positive impression on the company's top prospects.

12. False: Writing down a marketing communications plan is a waste of time. I know what needs to be done.

True: This belief can be fatal, particularly in companies where sales are driven or supported by marketing communications. Lack of a written plan can lead to sporadic efforts, frequent changes in direction, and impulsive expenditures. Most business owners know what needs to be done, but it's difficult under pressure to remember when, why, or even how without a written plan. To keep marketing communications—and the sales that depend on them—on track, create a simple written plan with assigned dates for implementation of your tactics.

13. False: With so many other expenses, marketing expenditures will just have to wait.

True: It's amazing how some businesspeople can give a higher priority to nearly anything other than marketing. Only when they believe their businesses are failing do they finally turn to marketing efforts in which they might have engaged months or years before. Sales and marketing communications are a top priority to any new business, particularly to home-based businesses starting with no name recognition, image, prominent location, or established following. Along with budgets for the basic tools and equipment required to perform one's work, sales and marketing budgets are the first order of business.

14. False: All my biggest competitors advertise in the Monday business section of the newspaper. I'll run my ad on Tuesday so it'll get noticed.

True: This can be a big mistake. A search corridor vehicle is created when the bulk of the advertisers for one product or service run in a given location on a designated day. That means when a prospect has made the decision to buy, he or she will look to the search corridor media for information on where to make that purchase. So, by placing an ad elsewhere, the advertiser loses the opportunity to speak to his hottest prospects. In the case of the business section of the daily newspaper, for example, readers may in fact peruse the section seven days a week, but use it as a tool for making buying decisions only on the designated day when competitive advertising is heaviest.

15. **False: I'm so busy this month, it's best to postpone sales and marketing activities for now.**

True: Home-based business owners who engage in sales and marketing communications activities only in the slow times may in fact be causing the up-and-down shifts in income for their firms. It's easy to get caught up in the day-to-day demands of doing the "work." But sustained growth may depend on staffing or structuring a home-based business to foster new business development. Sales and marketing communications should be undertaken consistently or according to a plan which anticipates a buildup in activity to support sales during slower periods.

16. **False: I'm sure there's a market for this product/service.**

True: Being sure and making sure are two different things. Too often, businesses are started on a hunch or supposition which research and analysis do not bear out. It's always best to test and study both the product or service and its potential market before launching any new business.

17. **False: My major competitors use videos to present. So I've got my brother's friend working on a video for me at a special price. That way, I can compete toe-to-toe.**

    True: When it comes to sales presentations, quality is important. A poorly produced video will look even worse when compared with big-budget videotapes produced by major competitors. In a competitive pitch situation, it's always best to stand out from the crowd by using a presentation method or style all one's own.

18. **False: Bigger is better.**

    True: This is what large companies competing with home-based businesses would like everyone to believe. Unfortunately for them, when it comes to such things as competitive pricing, top-quality work, conscientious service, and senior-level knowledge and expertise, today's home-based businesses are making big business look bad. In many ways, small is beautiful. This is evident even in the country's largest corporations which are restructuring divisions into smaller groups, units, cells, or task forces to improve quality and customer service.

Write Your Own Success Story

Your personal goal may well be to grow your home-based business into a major corporation. Indeed, sources suggest one in every five companies located in an office or industrial area began as a home-based business, including many major U.S. corporations such as Ford and Apple Computer. Or, you may wish to have fourteen or fewer employees like the vast majority of all American companies. But it will be your choice, and today your options are greater than ever.

Home-based businesses are changing the face of small business in America. Some might say this type of business ownership is the contemporary version of living over the store. But this analogy is in some ways incomplete. Today's home-based business owner is better educated and more affluent than the typical American worker and is not content to accept outmoded definitions of success. For many home-based business owners, success means providing a product or service you can be proud of, running a profitable business which yields a good income, and doing work you enjoy which provides a fine quality of life to be shared with family and friends.

Yet no matter how you define success, it's clear that home-based business ownership is just plain good for you, satisfying professional and personal needs while allowing for greater enjoyment of life and work. It's also good for the country, placing less stress on the environment and reducing pressure on America's infrastructure.

Though none of us can safely predict what effect this nationwide movement away from the traditional workplace will have in the next twenty or thirty years, in the here and now home-based business owners are thriving—no longer bound by traditional circumstances and definitions. And with unlimited opportunities for success.

INDEX

Q

R